THE

PROMETHEUS

CONNECTION

To Malcolm [illegible]
May the torch light
your way
Warmest
wishes
Kevin Osborne

A NOTE TO THE READER

To help our promotional efforts, your input— how you discovered this book— would be much appreciated. Please take a minute, tell us at

PrometheusConnection.com

(Your name, your email – not requested)

THE PROMETHEUS CONNECTION

America's Original Spirit:

Rise, Demise, Recovery

Mutekikon Publications

First Edition Published by Mutekikon Publications
Editor: Alex Bleier (v9)

Also available in Kindle format

Visit www.PrometheusConnection.com to find out more about the book and to connect to the author, the editor, and other "New Intellectuals" in their quest for America's Second Enlightenment.

Dedicated to all champions of reason-based defiance — past, present, and to come

Table of Contents

PREFACE & ACKNOWLEDGEMENTS

I depart from standard literary practice in combining two elements that usually stand apart.

This is done for a reason. I cannot adequately explain the evolution of this work without pointing to my inspirations. But inspiration alone will not bring a book into actual, tangible, physical reality. *That* endeavor is too complex. Too arduous. And so I want to salute my cast of support characters at the same time. I want them to be integral to this preface.

The Prometheus Connection started life back in my early 30's. I had become fascinated with Aristotle's conception of *megalopsychia* (greatness of soul), and it became the subject of my doctoral dissertation. I knew that *spirit*, understood in the completely natural (i.e. non-supernatural) sense of Aristotle and Ayn Rand and some of the other greats, is what underlies anything of importance in life.

Much later, studying America's history, I was struck by her early founding spirit and the fact that it is largely lost. Eventually I came to realize its connection to the Prometheus myth, especially in the hands of the great Aeschylus. Prometheus became the motif that really brought America's history to life for me. It was relatively clear sailing from that point on.

Many are the influences on the journey. For inspiration:

- The great-souled man of Aristotle's Nichomachean Ethics
- The invincible spirit of Aeschylus's Prometheus and America's Founding Fathers
- The inextinguishable flame of human reason
- The genius, Ayn Rand, who was, far and away, its greatest-ever champion
- The college professor who so long ago infected me with love of philosophy, Leonard Peikoff
- The titans and giants of American industry who have made so much possible
- The invincible spirit of Rostand's Cyrano, who cried to the universe, "Bring me Giants!"

For support:

- Bill Sims, scholar, whose pointed inputs rescued me from some ill-advised and less-than-compelling formulations
- Alex Bleier whose skilled editing helped me see material that did not belong, and whose glowing spirit so often buoyed me.
- Judy Stewart, beloved wife, with whom my life started, whose quiet flame is always there
- Jutta Hagen, friend and art master, who always urges me simply to see what is before my eyes
- Gary Wolf who took the time and reminded me of the long-ago Arab Renaissance
- Gen LaGreca whose encouraging words came at a time I most needed them.

Special mention must go to one person in particular in the above cast of sterling players. It is one thing to write a book. It is quite another actually to market and promote it. The latter, to me, are even more daunting than the actual writing.

To my great good fortune, however, my friend Alex Bleier, after reading the final manuscript, offered to do the technical heavy-lifting and take a lead role in publicizing the results. Amazon is revolutionary, Kindle and Print-On-Demand are marvels, social media and e-commerce are so very powerful, but I was not inclined to commit the time required to properly exploit them. Now in my later years, there is writing to do—always beckoning—a seductress not to be denied—ever envious of any other suitor.

You would not be holding *The Prometheus Connection* in your hands, or viewing it on your device, were it not for the genius of Alex Bleier and his magnanimous spirit.

Finally, as *The Prometheus Connection* evolved, it grew smaller. I continually condensed it down to barest essentials. But I provide ample endnotes to point the reader to back-up material and to further detail—*should he or she be interested.* In this Internet age, further study is never more than a click away.

Prologue

But Prometheus, whose name means "forethought," sees a way to defy Zeus. He cuts a giant fennel stalk, fashions it into a torch and after using it to steal the divine fire, brings it to mankind. Man, when touched by the fire, is suddenly no longer dependent on the gods to survive. Now he is lit by reason and thought. Before Prometheus, only the gods possessed such power. As punishment for this audacious theft, Zeus chains Prometheus to a desolate mountaintop and sends an eagle each day to feed on his liver. But his liver grows whole again at night, so that this hideous torture seems destined to last forever. Until, finally, after thousands of years, Heracles, the son of Zeus, slays the eagle and frees Prometheus.

Paraphrased from
Aeschylus's *Prometheus Bound*
[5th BC]
& other sources

Introduction

There are many masterworks of the imagination in human history and among those exhibiting the greatest impact and sweep are the ones dealing with the Ancient Greek myth of Prometheus.

A large body of scholarship and artistic expression across a number of cultures has been the result. Scholars analyze, compare, and contrast the many versions. They relate them to figures such as Jesus and creation myths such as the biblical fall of man. Paintings abound of Prometheus in chains. Sculptures stand in New York's Rockefeller Center and the Louvre in Paris. Musicians find inspiration, poets the muse, novelists and movie makers find raw material in the image. In a word, Prometheus the fire-bringer is ubiquitous.

The titan's universal appeal is not hard to understand, so evocative is his story: the sheer grandeur of it, the graphic detail, the diabolical nature of his punishment. But more important is Prometheus as the towering icon, the hero who brought the divine spark to mankind and, without hesitation, transgressed into the realm of the gods to do so.

There is the symbolism of the fire itself which so readily, especially in the powerful text of the genius known to us as Aeschylus, represents the spark of human consciousness, the animating spirit, the phenomenon of self-awareness which sets man apart from all other animals, and, yes, makes him somehow divine—god-like.

Then there is the underlying cosmic theme that overreaching action, pride, and defiance in the face of established authority are not to go unpunished. This added dimension—punishment—historically stands as the primary inspiration for most of the visual art dealing with the Prometheus myth. It also explains why Prometheus still connects so readily to the human condition now in the third millennium after he was first conceived.

This cosmic theme plays out on a grand scale for two aspects of America's history. First, there was the great controversy in the new republic over the role of God, specifically over church-state separation.[1] America, many

Christians claimed, defied the Christian God by ratifying a godless constitution, a transgression for which it has been made to suffer ever since—justifiably, they would say.

Second, late in the Western Enlightenment, a distant cluster of British colonies, with scant military means, rose up against the world's greatest power and was victorious. It then proceeded to form a new government which, in effect, deified the individual, declaring his right to life, liberty, property, and the pursuit of happiness. Then it had the audacity to limit the new government to the protection of those rights, explicitly relegating it to the service of that "deified" individual. Many have claimed that such defiance can only invite the wrath of established authority.

The subtitle of this work refers to *demise*. If America's founding spirit was essentially one of Promethean-like defiance, then Prometheus is now in chains.

The spirit that animated America at the time of her founding, and for the century and a half following, is *not* the spirit of today's America. The defiant founding spirit was suspicious of the historical tyranny of religion; today greater than fifty percent of the population believes church-state separation is not important. The defiant founding spirit was suspicious of the historical tyranny of government; today, by contrast, Americans—even many of those who protest such tyranny—seem ever more compliant in the face of government authority.

Passion for individual rights, so evident in our Founders, is today replaced by fervor for group rights. At the time of our founding, there existed a reverence for the individual; in countless ways today, the individual is subordinated to the group, so that the very concept, *individual,* appears to be disappearing.

During the Enlightenment, in Europe and in America, there was a reverence for reason, a belief that its power was unlimited. Today, we live in an age dominated by unreason and, often, outright irrationalism.

Early America exhibited great confidence in science and technology to improve human life; today basic science is poorly taught in our schools, and in many schools it is not taught at all. Technology, the offspring of basic science, is widely viewed as a danger to life, with man, the developer of technology, viewed as a "marauder" on the planet.[2]

In early America there was, for the most part, optimism about human nature, exhilaration in being free, and ambition to improve man's lot. In today's America, a spirit of nihilism and cynicism is all too real, succinctly captured by a late twentieth century movie, in which the lead character summarized American culture with, "It's all about bucks, kid. The rest is conversation." Then, as now, most Americans agree with this characterization of their country.[3]

By contrast, America's founding fire was ignited by the Enlightenment vision of what is possible to man and then fueled by passion, reason, reverence, confidence, optimism, exhilaration, and so many other markers of a free, vibrant, and flourishing culture. If we view those markers as manifestations of defiant *Promethean* fire, then that fire, early now in the third millennium, would have to be regarded as sputtering.

In this short work, the first two chapters outline and explain the rise of America's defiant Promethean spirit. Chapters three to five recount the demise of that spirit and why it was inevitable. Chapter six focuses on a twentieth century "Heracles," who essentially unleashed Prometheus again on the world and served, in the process, as an intellectual catalyst for the recovery of America's original spirit. The final chapter, number seven, advances a vision of how this recovery will lead to a Second American Enlightenment, a Second Age of Reason.

Prometheus the fire-bringer is the leitmotif of what follows. His story is rich in metaphor: Prometheus as the archetype of defiance, his torch as the symbol of reason and thought, Zeus as the great symbol of authority, chains as the tool used by authority to suppress defiance, Heracles as liberator.

All of these, along with the cosmic theme regarding overreaching action, can be drawn upon to illuminate America's complex history—past, present, and to come. The short "odyssey" on which you are about to begin explores and mines this theme and its associated metaphors.[4]

[1] I capitalize God whenever my reference is to the God of Christianity.

[2] Carl Sagan and Ann Druyan refer to "marauding high-technology civilizations" in *Shadows of Forgotten Ancestors* (New York: Ballantine Books, 1992), p. 364.

[3] Stanley Weiser and Oliver Stone, screenplay, *Wall Street* (Twentieth Century Fox: 1987), actor Michael Douglas speaking for lead character Gordon Gecko.

[4] I use the Aeschylus *Prometheus* in this work. Some modern scholars contest his authorship though, reportedly, scholars at the great library of Alexandria, significantly closer in time to the historical Aeschylus, unanimously gave the attribution to him. For the purpose of this short book, the issue is irrelevant.

I. Prometheus and America

The history of civilization is a mere blink in the vastness of time but is nonetheless an epic story of the human spirit triumphing over darkness. Historians mark that epic through the ages of stone, bronze, and iron. They call our attention to the birth of agriculture, of sea trade, and the golden age of exploration. Whatever the perspective, we see man emerging from the darkness of ignorance and confronting the physical world—upright and unafraid.

Aeschylus's Prometheus

Aeschylus, more than two and a half millennia ago in Ancient Greece, was aware of the arc of progress, although the ages just cited were only to become clearly discernable to later historians. But he made a significant contribution which sprang from a perspective typical of the Greek thinker of his day.

Aeschylus sought the *why* of progress, the *root*. That is, he sought to explain it. And this he did in *Prometheus Bound*, his great drama. Aeschylus's explanation was eloquent and emphatic, and he was among the first to advance it in such explicit terms.[5]

The Power to Think: Prometheus, his literary offspring, was Aeschylus's mouthpiece. It was Prometheus who stole the fire from the gods and brought it to mankind to dispel ignorance.

It was Prometheus who gave man the "power to think." "Through me," Prometheus proudly announces, men "won their minds" and the ability to create "all arts, all goods." They lifted themselves out of the darkness, learned to build shelters, and learned "the stars that tell the seasons," and number, "that most excellent device ... and letters joined in words." They also learned "the gift of healing" and so much else.[6]

Prometheus's words make Aeschylus's thinking clear. It does not require interpretation. It was man's mind, vividly symbolized by the fire stolen from the gods that made possible the dispelling of darkness. It was man's mind that gave him the ability to create all that made him civilized. It was man's mind that enabled him to triumph over his physical world.

The Supremacy of Mind: For the Greeks of antiquity the mind was supreme and, as Edith Hamilton expressed it, this supremacy "came to birth in Greece and lived in Greece alone in the ancient world." The Greeks, she states, "were the first intellectualists."[7]

This supremacy of mind and reason ruled in Greece for a scant several centuries, but that was sufficient time. Everything the Greeks explored was never seen in the same light again.

They sought to understand the physical world and were the first to do so without reference to the supernatural—and so they invented science. They brought reason to bear on observation—and so they invented the scientific method. They explored living beings—the science of biology—and identified what made man unique: mind and rational thought.

The Greeks invented the discipline known as philosophy and reveled in politics, one of its main branches. Here they explored the concept of freedom and the possibility that men in society could put aside force and, instead, deal with each other through reasoned discourse in peaceful assembly.

In ethics, another main branch of philosophy, they were the first to secularize morality, removing it from the hands of the priests.

They identified and championed *eudaimonia*, the flourishing life lived in the pursuit of excellence—in all things. And *megalopsychia*, greatness of soul, the crown of the moral man who has achieved that excellence in all virtues.[8]

Truly they glorified man on this earth, with one hand squeezing every last drop out of life, with the other hand holding high the torch of reason and thought—the torch of Prometheus.[9]

EUROPE'S DARK ERA

The Grip of Fundamentalism: Ancient Greece had great influence on the Roman civilization that followed, but after the Greco-Roman fall, more than a millennium passed before Europe again took up Prometheus's torch.

During those dark centuries, Europe was in the grip of fundamentalist Christianity.

The world was one of indescribable squalor, filth, and disease. Oppression was the rule, by church and feudal baron, by thief and murderer. Popes especially, as described by historian William Manchester, were "undisciplined by piety" and displayed unspeakable brutality.[10]

Mindlessness and Degradation: It was a time of superstition, endless fear, and "almost impenetrable mindlessness."[11] The Promethean fire of human reason and thought was not extinguished, but, by contrast to Greek antiquity, it was barely flickering. Human degradation was rife. The typical peasant bedstead was "piled high with straw pallets, all seething with vermin. Everyone slept there, regardless of age or gender—grandparents, parents, children, grandchildren, and hens and pigs." And this was the bedstead of *prosperous* peasants.[12]

A dismal concept of man prevailed during this long period, famously described by St. Augustine in the fifth century as "crooked and defiled, bespotted and ulcerous."[13] This father of the young Christian Church would no doubt have viewed the bedstead just described as a fitting place for such a creature to lay his head.

The European Enlightenment

The Great About-Face: If we leap to the beginning of the eighteenth century, however, a strikingly different concept of man had arisen. It was the period of the Enlightenment.

Enlightenment man was viewed as a noble creature, capable of achieving greatness through reason's power; even perfection was possible to him. How did this astounding reversal occur?

Aristotle's Role: To make it intelligible, we need to remember that the Promethean fire had never been fully extinguished in Europe. Scholastic monks kept it lit across the centuries.

Above all, however, it was two Dominican theologians of the 13th century who reached back, retrieved the torch of Prometheus, and fanned its flame.

They were the major intellects we know as Albertus Magnus and Thomas Aquinas.[14]

They became fervent champions of Aristotle—Aristotle, the ancient Greek natural philosopher and greatest advocate for human reason then known to man.[15]

This account, of course, condenses much history. But once again, the torch of Prometheus touched mankind. Once again, reason was unleashed on the world, triggering an explosion of natural philosophy and science and producing an enormous secularizing effect.

From that point, Europe's progression away from the medieval darkness was steady. It was agonizing at times but steady overall. It was a grand history, a history of a great about-face in Western man's view of man.

The end result was the flowering known as The Enlightenment.[16]

The American Enlightenment

Two millennia after Aeschylus, during the infancy of its Enlightenment, Europe began colonizing a "new" land across the Atlantic. The early settlers came to a harsh place, endured unimaginable hardship, and suffered death in great numbers during the early years as they clawed their way to a new life.

But great courage and grit enabled them to survive without breaking and, eventually, two hundred years after their first arrival, they created a new government. It was late in the 18th century.

During the two previous centuries, however, there had occurred a momentous development. Enlightenment ideas which had swept Europe and flourished had quite naturally found their way to the colonies. We need to pause here, for this development was enormously significant for the future of the North American continent.

The Enlightenment, more than any other development, carried the torch of Prometheus, the torch of reason and thought, into what was to become a new republic.

A Secular Philosophy: Enlightenment ideas implicitly set forth a philosophy, a *secular* philosophy, on which the founding of America was based. This was the philosophy which produced the spirit of our Founding Fathers and supplanted that of the Church father, Augustine.

From its earliest days, America imported a great deal from Europe: people, religions, and, eventually, early in the century of its founding, the ideas of the European Enlightenment. Indeed, the new republic, a *constitutional* republic, would not have happened, let alone taken the form it did, without Enlightenment ideas. Their significance cannot be overemphasized, not only those ideas that were imported, but those of American intellectuals as well. As one historian explains, "the thinkers of the Enlightenment in America made a distinctive contribution which is worthy of examination in and of itself."[17]

The Sovereignty of Human Reason: The philosophy of the Enlightenment defied the Christian God, as fully as Prometheus defied Zeus.

During the Enlightenment, the power of intelligence and human reason replaced dependence on God. To Enlightenment intellectuals, the universe was seen as lawful, orderly, and intelligible without reference to supernatural intervention.

In human life, reason was sovereign and, aided by observation and the scientific method, it was believed capable of knowledge, certainty, and truth. Individual man was given primacy over the group, and the concept of government as man's servant, responsible for protecting his natural rights, had come into being.[18]

America's Founders were well schooled in these ideas. They were educated men who were passionate about the right to life, liberty, property, and the pursuit of happiness. They understood that a life without these principles was intolerable and that only a tyrannical government would violate them. So eloquent were they in expressing these ideas, that America is defined to this day by its founding documents. The Declaration of Independence and the Constitution—short as they are—remain as foundations.

And so the great experiment which was America had its beginning. Though it was not without contradictions, nonetheless it was a constitutional republic the likes of which the world had not seen before or since.[19]

An Age of Giants: The history of America's founding is marked by drama, agony, and inspiration: the years leading to the Declaration of Independence, the Revolutionary War battles and the constitutional conventions and ratification. Some historians see a near epic grandeur to this history, worthy of Aeschylus's Prometheus.

This is an age of giants, of intellectually-minded men of action, who truly stood to lose everything. Cassara's description of "the man of thought in action" is eloquently simple and accurate.[20] These are heroes who put their lives and their way of life on the line for their beliefs, "mutually" pledging "to each other," in the final words of the Declaration of Independence, their "Lives," their "Fortunes" and their sacred "Honor."

The capitalized words are in the original to emphasize their importance. And of great significance, Jefferson added the concept "sacred" to one of them—*honor*—that supreme quality of soul—an absolute never to be compromised. Only giants—*spiritual* giants—would think this way.

A Nation of Principle: Revisionists sometimes claim that many of the founding revolutionaries were rich property owners motivated simply by the wish to preserve their "fortunes." But, actually, such men tend to shrink from the steely, implacable resolve required for true revolution.

They are the kind of men Thomas Paine no doubt would include under his scornful labels "summer soldier" and "sunshine patriot" in his fiery pamphlet. They were the men who would shrink from a fight to the death for freedom because, in their souls, they hold something else, such as material possessions, more dear than freedom.[21]

The end result of the American Revolution was that for the first time in human history, a nation was founded explicitly on the principle of individual rights, explicitly on the concept of freedom. This was the unique contribution to history of the American Enlightenment.[22]

AMERICA'S ORIGINAL SPIRIT

Men of Passion: America's Founders were passionate men. George Washington, Thomas Jefferson, James Madison, Benjamin Franklin, John Adams, Patrick Henry, Thomas Paine—their stories, and those of so many other "worthies," are forever burned into the record of America's founding.

They had that special quality of soul, honed to an exquisitely fine pitch, that was necessary to take great ideas—radical, audacious, revolutionary—and translate them into physical reality, in the face of what was then the greatest military power in history. They had courage, conviction, and an underlying spirit that fueled both.[23]

The Fuel of the Revolution: What was that underlying spirit of America's Founders? What was the underlying spirit of those men for whom ideas were all important, so important that life without them was intolerable—so important that they were willing to risk everything to secure them on this earth, or die trying?

The answer fairly leaps from the previous paragraphs. Defiance was the original spirit of America. Described in physical terms, it was a solid *rock* of defiance.

But this does not really capture its essence. Above all, it was an *intellectual* defiance in the face of tyrannical authority.

In short, it was *reason-based*.

The Founding Fathers defiantly flung reason into the face of faith and superstition. They separated religion from public affairs, making it, instead, strictly a matter of private conscience.

The Founding Fathers defiantly hurled individual rights into the face of institutionalized servitude. They formed a limited government, a republic, subservient to the individual, and flung it into the face of an all-powerful government, Great Britain.

Intellectual defiance of tyrannical authority, that is, defiance based on reason and principle, is what fueled their courage in the face of the very real possibility of a violent death. And, as history gives witness, that indeed was the fate of many of them.

Prometheus and America

When we talk about early America and its founding, we are talking about another age, another era. We are talking about the Age of Reason in America.

We are also talking about an age of honor—*sacred* honor.

It was an era in which men expressed passion for their values. It was an era lit by passion for excellence.

The ancient Greek mindset had returned. That mindset, so forcefully exhibited by Aeschylus, produced Prometheus and then a cast of brilliant philosophers, culminating in the most brilliant of them all, Aristotle.

It also produced America.

Both cultures—Ancient Greece and revolutionary America—were fired by the torch of Prometheus—that timeless symbol of the human mind, of reason, of thought—that timeless symbol of intellectual defiance and intellectual freedom.

Man at his best.

---

[5] According to H. D. F. Kitto, such myths are "among the supreme achievements of the human mind, dramas about the birth and growth of reason, order and mercy among gods and men alike." See *The Greeks,* Revised Edition (London: the Penguin Group, 1991), p. 202.

It should be pointed out that, though Aeschylus did not originate the myth of Prometheus the fire-bringer, his unique version is the one I use.

[6] Translation by Edith Hamilton, *The Prometheus Bound of Aeschylus*, in *Three Greek Plays,* (New York: W. W. Norton & Company, 1937), pp.115-117, *passim*.

[7] Edith Hamilton, *The Greek Way*, Special Edition, (New York: Time Inc., 1963), p 6.

[8] *Eudaimonia* was most famously treated in Aristotle's *Nichomachean Ethics*, Bk. X, Ch. 6 and 7. And *megalopsychia*, in the same work, Book IV, Ch. 3, exalts the completely moral man.

[9] Edith Hamilton, *op. cit.*, in the first two chapters, pp. 2-35, eloquently elaborates this, in her uniquely passionate style.

[10] William Manchester, *A World Lit Only By Fire,* (Boston: Little, Brown And Company, 1993), p. 42.

[11] *Ibid.*, p.3.

[12] *Ibid.*, p. 53.

[13] Edward Bouverie Pusey trans., Augustine's *Confessions*, Bk. 8, Ch. 7, in vol. 18, *Great Books of the Western World*, (Chicago: Encyclopedia Britannica, Inc., 1952). See also http://www.ourladyswarriors.org/saints/augcon7.htm#chap21 , accessed January 30, 2013.

The words quoted are Augustine's self-assessment but, as the context makes clear, are meant by him to apply to human nature generally.

---

[14] For this period see Friedrich Heer, *The Medieval World*, (Cleveland: The World Publishing Company, 1961), especially pp. 216-234 for his treatment of Thomas Aquinas.

[15] Aristotle's six works on logic comprise what scholars designate his *Organon.* For his famous three laws of logic, see his *Metaphysics*, Book IV, Parts 4 and 7. Aristotle's influence cannot be overstressed.

[16] Heer, *op. cit.*, p. 219, refers to Thomas Aquinas as the "father of the Enlightenment," but Thomas, given his reverence for the man he called "The Philosopher," would no doubt, were he a historian looking back today, have reserved the term, "Father of the Enlightenment," for Aristotle himself.

[17] Ernest Cassara, *The Enlightenment in America,* (Boston: Twayne Publishers, 1975), p. 22. Cassara's 208 page book is a concise history of the subject, marvelously lucid on key aspects, e.g. the lifestyle of the enlightened American, pursuit of science, the rights of man, and what he refers to as the "quasi-religion" of deism.

[18] The role of philosopher and political thinker, John Locke [1632-1704] cannot be overemphasized. See Edward Cline, "John Locke and Liberty," first published in the Spring 1999 issue of the *Journal of Colonial Williamsburg*, and subsequently in McGraw-Hill/Dushkin's *Western Civilization II* college textbook in September 2000 and again in September 2002.

Cline's essay is available in its entirety at, among other places, http://www.familysecuritymatters.org/publications/detail/john-locke-and-liberty.

[19] By far, the most glaring contradiction was the savage curse of slavery. This inhuman scourge, though beyond excusing, does not diminish the fundamental ideals of the Founding Fathers.

In fact, these are the ideals which, in the end, established legal equality for all, and now, long after official abolition, enable society to address the residual racism that, shamefully, still remains.

The great visionary, Dr. Martin Luther King Jr., recognized these ideals in his "I Have a Dream" speech, http://www.americanrhetoric.com/speeches/mlkihaveadream.htm.

See also Michael A. LaFerrara, "Martin Luther King Jr. and the Fundamental Principle of America," *The Objective Standard*, http://www.theobjectivestandard.com/blog/index.php/2013/01/martin-luther-king-jr-and-the-fundamental-principle-of-america/, January 21, 2013 blog entry.

[20] Cassara, *op. cit.,* p. 34.

[21] Thomas Paine, *The Crisis*, first of 16 pamphlets, (Pennsylvania: Read aloud on Dec. 23, 1776 to the soldiers of the Continental Army.

In the next three days they crossed the Delaware River to fight and win the Battle of Trenton.) Full text: http://www.ushistory.org/paine/crisis/c-01.htm.

[22] See Leonard Peikoff, *The Ominous Parallels*, (New York: Stein and Day, 1982), Ch. 5, "The Nation of the Enlightenment," pp. 101-118. My treatment owes much to Peikoff's luminous account of the period.

[23] "Founding Fathers of the United States," *Wikipedia The Free Encyclopedia*, http://en.wikipedia.org/wiki/Founding_Fathers_of_the_United_States, provides a list of links to concise biographies (with vivid images) of the players mentioned and also that of many other founding figures. Last modified July 9, 2014.

II. Reason Unbound

Ancient Greece and Enlightenment America upheld human reason as a preeminent value. For each culture that reality was all-defining.

In the case of America, even the deadly action—or *especially* the deadly action—to which her Founders committed themselves was pursued in the name of human reason. It was *principled* action. At its core, their defiance of the historical tyrannies of God and King was an *intellectual* defiance grounded on the principle of individual rights.

This defiance, however, was not shared by the entire population. Nor was it shared by all intellectuals. Some urged caution rather than outright revolution.

But the Founding Fathers, passionate about freedom, ultimately prevailed. The strength of their convictions had a moral fervor that was unstoppable. And, contrary to the opinion of some historians, it was shared by the great majority of the colonists, and not merely by a minority group of radical intellectuals.[24]

Reason, rational thought, dedication to freedom carried the day—and the period. They also carried the next great period.

Another revolution was about to begin. This time it was a peaceful one.

America's Industrial Revolution

The Challenge: For the beginning of the story, we need to consider America's situation immediately after winning independence. The essence of it was this: *America's survival was less than certain*.

As writers Nothhaft and Kline put it, the economy was essentially a backward agrarian one, dependent on imports, and supported by a meager population of barely three million. By contrast, England's population was nine million.

As they go on to explain, however, the new country had strengths. She had abundant, though untapped, natural resources and a population that doubled every twenty years, the fastest rate in the world. And this population, though relatively small and lacking higher education, was largely literate.

Above all, as a publisher of the time stated, it was a population imbued with "a universal ambition to go forward."[25] This, of course, reflected the optimistic Enlightenment mindset of the age.

The Founders, nonetheless, were faced with a great challenge. How should the new nation leverage its assets to best jump-start a primitive economy? This was the question taken up by the Constitutional Convention as it began its proceedings in 1787 Philadelphia.

A Revolutionary Patent System: To start, the Founders looked to the patent system of England, the country then leading the Industrial Revolution. But as they looked, they quickly saw that England's patent system had limitations.

Securing patents often depended on court connections, making them vulnerable to revocation or expropriation without compensation. Patent application fees were so high that only the wealthy could afford them. Laws limited the ability of inventors to sell or license the rights to their inventions. Thus, unless they enjoyed great wealth, inventors lacked the capital needed to commercialize their inventions.[26]

As economic historians, Lamoreaux and Sokoloff put it, the framers of America's patent system wanted to avoid such limitations. Instead, their vision was a patent system that would unleash the entrepreneurial energy of *ordinary* people. The 1787-1788 constitution and the laws promulgated from it accomplished exactly that.[27]

It started with Article one section eight which declares that Congress shall have the power to "promote the Progress of Science and useful Arts, by securing for limited Times to Authors and Inventors the exclusive Right to their respective Writings and Discoveries."

A simple statement, yet it was revolutionary. It was the first time the constitution of any nation included an intellectual property clause.[28]

The patent system that grew out of this revolutionary statement was exceedingly friendly to inventors. Lamoreaux and Sokoloff explain the dynamics. Patent fees were set so low that any ordinary citizen could afford them. Patent application procedures were greatly simplified.

Examination of a patent application by technical experts for novelty and conformity with statutes reduced uncertainty about the validity and value of an invention. This made it easier for the inventor to sell or license his invention and thus realize a monetary return.

From the first patent law of 1790, Lamoreaux and Sokoloff continue, America's patent system "included provisions explicitly designed to support trade in patent rights, and both the courts and U.S. Patent Office acted to facilitate such transfers."[29] Also, enforcement of patent rights, they state, was assigned to the federal courts where "judges quickly developed an effective set of principles for protecting the rights of patentees and also of those who purchased or licensed patented technologies."[30]

Nothhaft and Kline stress that the promotion of patents as *tradable assets* was a wholly unique feature of the American patent system, spurring a dramatic rise in the per capita patenting rate. In 1865, they report, it was triple that of Great Britain.

Even more dramatic was that by 1880 eighty-five percent of American patents were licensed by their inventors, in contrast to only thirty percent in England.[31] Lamoreaux and Sokoloff report that even as early as 1810, "despite its lag in industrial development, the United States far surpassed Britain in patenting per capita."[32]

The Patent System's Key Role: We need to pause and consider the significance of the new country's patent system. It cannot be overemphasized. It gave to writers and inventors *exclusive* right to their writing and their inventions. The framers realized that not only does writing involve intellectual property but inventing does too. Writers have the copyright system to secure their intellectual property; inventors have the patent system to secure *their* intellectual property. Laws promulgated from Article one section eight of the constitution accomplished this in each case.

A patent, once issued, secures intellectual property in two ways. First, it legally certifies to the world that the inventor was the originator of the idea behind the invention. Second, the patent system protects his exclusive right to profit from that invention—to reproduce it—to *commercialize* it. This means that, during the limited term of the patent, it would be unlawful for anyone else to attempt to do so.

The impact of America's patent system on the new country was momentous. It was the first time in the history of economics that an ordinary person could make a living as an inventor. More than that, an ordinary person, simply by applying his reason and intelligence—and "street smarts"—could become prosperous.

An Explosion of Invention: The result was a riot of innovation. Philosopher Andrew Bernstein concisely captures it. "The 19th century in America," he states, "was the single greatest era of technological and industrial advance in history." He points to the sewing machine, the steam elevator, the airbrake for railroad cars, the telegraph, the reaper, skyscrapers, suspension bridges, the conquering of typhoid and yellow fever, the camera, the phonograph, the electric light, the motion picture projector.

The 20th century, he continues, saw television and the revolution of transportation by automobile and airplane. Manufacturing was revolutionized by the "method of mass production that brought modern inventions to millions."[33] For each advance, there were ripple effects, triggering innovations in other sectors of the economy.

All these marvels are simply a few of the highlights. Truly, it was as if the new nation had been touched by the torch of Prometheus. America's Industrial Revolution was running full bore.

Titans: If the inventive geniuses of the time are regarded as giants, as well they should be, there was another class of producer for which even *that* term is inadequate. Instead, we need the term reserved for the demigods of Greek literature, of whom Prometheus was one—*Titans*. To this day, this is the term applied to Andrew Carnegie (1835-1919: Steel), John D. Rockefeller (1839-1937: Oil), Cornelius Vanderbilt (1794-1887: Steamboats and Railroads), James J. Hill (1838-1916: Railroads), Edward H. Harriman (1848-1909: Railroads), J.P. Morgan (1837-1913: Banking and Finance).

As is well known, these figures and a number of others were vilified in their lifetime as "Robber Barons," and the period of American history they made possible invariably goes by the derogatory "Gilded Age."[34]

For now, however, I want simply to call attention to the Promethean nature of this cast of characters, for each, in his own way and in his own field, personified Prometheus. Each had enormous vision or foresight. Like Aeschylus's Prometheus, America's giants, as well as the super-giants or "titans," were proud of their achievements and the quality of their work.

Rockefeller, writing to one of his partners, remarked: "We must ... remember we are refining oil for the poor man and he must have it cheap and good."[35] James J. Hill, reflecting on his continent building, remarked "... we look back at what we have done and how we ... led all western companies in opening the country and carrying at the lowest rates ..."[36]

We read such statements and think of Aeschylus's Prometheus who declares, "None else but I first found the seaman's car, sail-winged, sea-driven, Such ways to help I showed them ..."[37]

A Meteoric Rise in Living Standard: The height of America's Industrial Revolution was roughly the period from the last third of the 19th into the early 20th century. Driven by titans of heavy industry and the inventive giants of lighter industry, America's living standard improved at an explosive rate.

Historians differ in their evaluation of it, but not over the fact that it occurred. As economist-financier Michael Dahlen summarizes, "from 1870 to 1910, real GDP increased at an average annual rate of 3.97 percent." America had surpassed Britain "as the world's leading industrial nation." During the same period, "consumer prices actually *declined* at an average annual rate of .16 percent" while, overall, "real wages in manufacturing doubled." Because the rates of improvement were *annual* rates, they were compounding. The improvement truly was staggering—titanic.[38]

Promethean Vision: As writer Alex Epstein reports, late in life, Rockefeller looked back and recalled, "We had vision. We saw the vast possibilities of the oil industry." He saw that his company had "stood at the center of it, and brought [its] knowledge and imagination and business experience to bear in a dozen, in twenty, in thirty directions."[39]

Rockefeller did not stand alone. Each titan of America's Industrial Revolution possessed towering vision—"vision," that synonym of "forethought," the literal translation of the Greek name "Prometheus."

Vision was the quality common to all the inventors and innovators of the age, uniting them through their myriad endeavors. It was this *vision* that changed the face of America.

Freedom and Rights

Freedom from Coercion: What were the conditions that made possible America's explosive growth during her first century and a half? In a word, it was *freedom*. But to be precise, it was *freedom* in the Enlightenment sense of the term. It was freedom from coercive authority.

The simple truth is this: America's business climate was one of freedom and respect for individual rights.

America's revolutionary patent system was the great exemplar of that fact, at the most elemental level. This was the level of innovation.

But the same was true on a wider political level. America's constitution provided a framework that made America's economy the freest economy in history, by a large margin.

As Michael Dahlen explains, in the first century and a half after her founding, America's economy was largely uncontrolled. The constitution protected private property with Amendment Five. It established sound currency through sections eight and ten of Article one, and it prohibited states from erecting trade barriers with section nine of the same article. Additionally, section eight severely limited the government's power to intervene in the marketplace.

Government's role in commerce was minimal, existing primarily to protect the right of voluntary trade, to prosecute any initiation of force (theft, fraud, breach of contract, copyright and patent infringements), and to arbitrate honest disagreement.

Other than the execution of such functions, government, for the most part, did not interfere. In short, America then was a different place from America now.

There were no federal regulatory agencies to dictate how goods were to be produced and traded. Exceptions existed—tariffs, national banking, infrastructure improvements—but were, as Dahlen puts it, "limited in scope and were accompanied by considerable debate about whether they should exist at all."

Private entrepreneurs, he reports, built most roads and many canals. When state governments intervened in the 1820's to subsidize canal building, most of those canals "went unfinished, generated little to no income, or went bankrupt."

Post Civil War, Dahlen continues, federal subsidies for the transcontinental railroads caused similar problems—as well as corruption." The most successful of the transcontinental railroads was James Jerome Hill's Great Northern which was built without any subsidies or land grants.[40]

Contrary to the implicit premise of the "Robber Baron" slur, men of this time were generally free to deal with one another on the basis of voluntary trade, using reason and not its antithesis, coercion. It was such economic freedom that drove America's Industrial Revolution.

A Respect for Rights: As we saw with America's patent system, the framers could have established impediments to innovation of the kind seen in Europe. Instead, they consciously avoided them.

They kept government out of the way of the inventor-entrepreneur and basically limited government to one function only. That function, so clearly stated by America's Founding Fathers, was the most important of all. That function was to secure and enforce individual rights. In the case of a patent, it was an inventor's exclusive right to his intellectual property—the intellectual property underlying his invention.

REASON UNBOUND

America is a product of two great historical movements. The first was the Enlightenment, covered in chapter one. The second was the Industrial Revolution, covered in this chapter. Together, these movements undergird and explain her founding and the shape into which she grew during her first century and a half.

Both movements show us America lit by the torch of Prometheus. Together they demonstrate the power of human reason and thought in the shaping of man's world. They also illustrate the power of vision and of freedom. Reason truly was unbound in America during her first 150 years.

The grand vision of the framers coupled with the focused vision of individual inventors provided the infrastructure for the towering vision of the business titans. Together these three catalysts—the framers, the inventors, the titans—drove the greatest and most rapid growth the world has ever seen—truly spectacular growth.

***

But there is more to the story. The Enlightenment was not to last in America. She remained the world's leading industrial power, but her original spirit was to change. America's history is a complicated history, a *very* complicated history. Zeus, Prometheus's nemesis, was not idle in America during her Enlightenment and Industrial Revolution.

---

[24] For a marvelous dramatization of the decades leading up to the Revolutionary War, see Edward Cline's six-novel *Sparrowhawk* series. The oppression of the American colonies was severe and extensive. Cline, with his penetrating knowledge of the time, both British and American, brings to life the widespread defiance of America's population. (Patrick Henry Press, Kindle available, http://www.amazon.com/s/ref=sr_gnr_fkmr1?rh=i%3Astrip-books%2Ck%3Acline+sparrowhawk&keywords=cline+sparrow-hawk&ie=UTF8&qid=1408192438

---

[25] Henry R. Nothhaft with David Kline, *Great again: revitalizing America's entrepreneurial leadership*, (Boston: Harvard Business Review Press, 2011), pp. 70-71. (The publisher mentioned was Hezekiah Niles.)

[26] *Ibid.,* p. 71.

[27] Naomi R. Lamoreaux and Kenneth L. Sokoloff, editors, *Financing Innovation in the United States, 1870 to the Present,* (Cambridge Massachusetts: The MIT Press, 2007), p. 4.

All references to Lamoreaux and Sokoloff in coming paragraphs are taken from their informative essay in this work, "Introduction: The Organization and Finance of Innovation in American History," pp. 1-37, which includes extensive notes and references.

[28] Nothhaft and Kline, *op. cit.,* p. 72.

[29] Lamoreaux and Sokoloff, *op. cit.,* p. 4.

[30] *Ibid*., p. 30, note 4. The authors also cite Zorina B. Khan, "Property Rights and Patent Litigation in Early Nineteenth-Century America," *Journal of Economic History,* 1995, pp. 55, 58-97, and Zorina B. Khan, *The Democratization of Invention: Patents and Copyrights in American Economic Development, 1790-1920,* (Cambridge: Cambridge University Press, 2005).

[31] Nothhaft and Kline, *op. cit*., p. 74.

[32] Lamoreaux and Sokoloff, *op. cit.,* p. 5.

[33] Andrew Bernstein, *Capitalist Manifesto,* (Lantham, Maryland: University Press of America, 2005), p. 138. Also see pp. 139-148 where Bernstein discusses the players involved, one by one.

[34] See "Robber Baron (Industrialist)," *Wikipedia The Free Encyclopedia*, last modified, June 23, 2014.
http://en.wikipedia.org/wiki/Robber_baron_(industrialist), for links to 26 "suspects," with a luminous "mug shot" of each.

Bernstein, *op. cit.,* pp. 395-438, comes to their defense, and in his endnotes, pp. 469-472, lists a large body of scholarship in the same vein.

For more on Andrew Carnegie specifically, see Yaron Brook and Don Watkins, "To Be Born Poor Doesn't Mean You'll Always Be Poor," *Forbes*, April 29, 2013, http://www.forbes.com/sites/objectivist/2013/04/12/to-be-born-poor-doesnt-mean-youll-always-be-poor/.

[35] Bernstein, *op. cit.*, p. 404.

Writer Alex Epstein points out that, by 1879, "Rockefeller controlled 90% of the refining market. According to antitrust theory," he continues, "this meant he could restrict output and force artificially high prices.

But the reality was somewhat different. By revolutionizing the method of producing refined oil, Rockefeller brought about an explosion of productivity, profit, and improvement to human life.

In the 1870's he "shrunk the cost of light by a factor of thirty, thereby adding hours to the days of millions around the world."

See "Vindicating Capitalism: The Real History of the Standard Oil Company," *The Objective Standard*, Vol. 3, No. 2, Summer 2008. http://www.theobjectivestandard.com/issues/2008-summer/standard-oil-company.asp, available as a PDF or free MP3 audio download.

[36] Bernstein, *op. cit.,* p. 413.

[37] Edith Hamilton, *The Prometheus Bound of Aeschylus,* in *Three Greek Plays,* (New York: W. W. Norton & Company, 1937), p.115.

[38] Michael Dahlen, "The Rise of American Big Government: A Brief History of How We Got Here," *The Objective Standard*, Vol. 4, No. 3, Fall 2009, http://www.theobjectivestandard.com/issues/2009-fall/rise-of-american-big-government.asp, available as a PDF download.

[39] Epstein, *op. cit.,* citing David Freeman Hawke, ed., *The William O. Inglis Interview with John D. Rockefeller, 1917-1920* (Westport, CT: Meckler Publishing, 1984), microfiche. Epstein captures many personal qualities of Rockefeller that are counter to the slur "Robber Baron."

---

[40] Dahlen, *op. cit.* traces this in detail. He also makes clear, however, that, from the beginning, America was not a fully free market, and he indicates the forces by which America has become progressively less free.

III. Zeus in America

America's original spirit was an implacable defiance of the age-old tyrannies of God and King. Chapters one and two dealt with the rise of this spirit, its precise nature, and the extraordinary flourishing it brought to the new nation.

That founding spirit, however, did not endure. Its demise soon followed, and concurrent with it was a resurgence of religion. We need to pause on religion in this chapter, for any discussion of American culture is incomplete without a full understanding of its role.

The Fading of the American Enlightenment

The Turn from Reason: In Enlightenment America, as in any Enlightenment country, man's nature was viewed as potentially noble and great—even perfectible—by virtue of the power of reason. By the end of America's first century and a half, however, the earlier Christian concept of human nature had largely returned. No longer was reason to be regarded as a preeminent value.

Why did America abandon Enlightenment reason so readily? In a word, we could say it was *inevitable*—which, in truth, it was. But we still need to understand why.

To start, we need to recall that the Enlightenment in America was originally a European import. It was largely a product of European thinking. Consequently, when the Enlightenment faded in Europe it *had* to fade in America as well.

Philosopher, Leonard Peikoff, explains the progression. America's Founders, he points out, were not themselves political philosophers. They seemed to take it for granted that Europe's thinkers had done the philosophic work to provide a firm intellectual base for Enlightenment principles.

But actually, as Peikoff puts it, they "were counting on what did not exist." Far from providing a solid foundation, European thought was, in his words, "torn by contradictions ... and eminently vulnerable to challenge."[41]

It was not long before Europe turned away from Enlightenment ideas and, when this happened, America gradually followed suit. It started at the beginning of the 19th century. As Peikoff summarizes, America's intellectuals, following Europe's lead, "turned increasingly against every one of America's founding ideas and ideals," and worked to "remake the United States in the image of the successive waves of European irrationalism."[42]

The image into which America's intellectuals remade America found two main expressions. One expression was secular—Pragmatism; the other was religious—Christianity.

The Philosophy of Pragmatism: Pragmatism originated in late 19th century America with Charles Pierce, William James and John Dewey. It is a largely American product.[43]

Enlightenment ideas, the pragmatist claims, were relevant once, but they are not immutable truths, good at all times and places. In fact, today, they are outdated.

As with any principle, the pragmatist continues, those of the Enlightenment simply waste mental energy. While Enlightenment thinkers viewed thinking as an essentially noble activity, John Dewey sees thinking as a disease, a view reflected in his influential views on education.

In addressing problems, the rational approach, says the pragmatist, is simply to ask what to do today to address them. Knowledge and certainty are not possible. Rather, we must simply look for those ideas that seem to work the best, by their consequences.

Pragmatism is diametrically opposed to Enlightenment philosophy, especially in the field of epistemology. The ideals of the Founding Fathers cannot be expected to survive in the pragmatist world. And in fact they do not.[44]

The "Philosophy" of Christianity: Christianity is the second expression of the image into which intellectuals remade America as the Enlightenment faded. Zeus had actually always been lurking in the background, but Enlightenment thought had been keeping him at bay. Once the Enlightenment waned, Zeus in his Christian incarnation was able to roam freely once again.

More theology than philosophy, Christianity nonetheless must be factored into any account of America's intellectual history.

America's Religious Scene

Long before the first settlers arrived from Europe, a native spiritual tradition prevailed in what was to become America. As with most native cultures throughout the world, most Native Americans believe in the immortality of the human spirit and in some kind of afterlife. In addition, most recognize an all-powerful and all-knowing Master Spirit, and they view the material and spiritual realms as unified, rather than disparate aspects of reality.[45]

Puritan Calvinism: Christianity, the focus of this chapter, is something quite different. Its original form in America was the Puritan Calvinism of the pilgrims.

This is a stark religion best known for such doctrines as the total depravity of human nature, predestination, faith as the primary means of knowledge, and man's absolute dependence on God for eternal life, and *not* good works. It was from this dark beginning that an enormous diversity within American Christianity was to evolve.[46]

A Riot of Variety: America's religious scene, as it evolved after the Puritan era, has always been wildly chaotic, ever changing, and fluid. There are hundreds of Protestant sects alone, from "Prosperity Gospelers" at one end of the spectrum to "New Calvinists" at the other.[47] In between, splinter groups abound, such as Charismatics and Pentecostals and the "Neo" variants of each.

Evangelicals are a large force on the religious Right and might be "traditionalists," "centrists," or "modernists." Additionally, they could be "Conservative," "Open," or "Post." Neo-Evangelicals also exist, as well as the Evangelical Left. Jimmy Carter, 39th president of the United States, falls squarely into this last camp, as does 44th president, Barak Obama, discussed later.[48]

Within mainline Protestantism, such as Methodists, Lutherans, Presbyterians, and Congregationalists, there is variation as well. And even within Catholicism, where the Vatican historically is a strong unifying force, various factions exist. This is especially the case after the upheavals of "Vatican II" in the latter half of the 20th century.[49]

There are also Christians who regard themselves as Nondenominational. But even within this "non-committed" group, there is noticeable variation.[50]

Then there are variations in how intensely people hold their beliefs and how fervently they practice them. Surveys regularly confirm that many Americans are not very fervent at all, preferring their religion "lite," a Sunday-morning-church-going activity, if even that.

People vary in what they choose to believe, preachers in what they preach, and politicians in how they answer the now-inevitable prying into their beliefs. Atheists and agnostics do not get elected in America. Nor do Republicans get elected without currying favor from the Religious Right, early now in the 21st century.

Why the Variety: It was the American Enlightenment, and the Constitution it led to, which enabled American religion to thrive so robustly. More than any other factor—and social commentators discuss them at length—it was the Constitution's "disestablishment" clause that led to the rampant flourishing of religion in America.

This famous clause is the portion of the First Amendment that reads, "Congress shall make no law respecting an establishment of religion, or prohibiting the free exercise thereof ...."

As one journalist succinctly puts it, America has a deep religious history but no established church. Consequently, it encourages "religious free-lancers and entrepreneurs." This nicely points to the business side of American religion and the fact that there is money to be made from it, as televangelists demonstrate so skillfully.[51]

In America, no religion was ever singled out for state protection. Instead, *any* religion—or even *no* religion—was allowed, and this was historically unprecedented. As the Enlightenment faded, freedom of religion in

America continued unabated, constitutionally enshrined and protected as, of course, it should be.

ORDER FROM THE CHAOS

Three Major Groups: Despite the seeming chaos of America's religious scene, there are ways to make it intelligible. To begin, we can break the 75% of America's adult population that claims to be Christian into three major groups.

Though statistics vary and receive much analysis as to significance, surveys regularly confirm that, early in the 21st century, Evangelical Protestants, Catholics, and mainline Protestants each account for roughly 25% of the entire American population. The remaining 25% is made up of non-Christians or a small percentage of non-believers (atheists and agnostics).

A Further Reduction: But an even greater simplification is possible. Instead of breaking Christianity into three major groups, we can reasonably divide Christianity into just *two* major groups: Mainline Christians (Catholics and various mainline Protestant denominations) accounting for 50% of the entire population of America, and Fundamentalists (largely Evangelical Protestants) accounting for the remaining 25%.

Core Beliefs of All Christians: Despite the enormous diversity of American Christianity, all Christians, with few exceptions, share the same core beliefs. These beliefs provide them with a distinct view of the world and of human nature, a morality of how humans are to live, and a position on how it is that humans know this.

Starting with the world view, it is dualistic. Christians believe that there is a perfect supernatural realm where God exists and an imperfect realm where humans prepare for eternity with Him in heaven.

In this endeavor, humans are inherently weak, even depraved as a result of the original fall in the Garden of Eden. But with volition and God's grace, Christians can overcome this weakness and live rightly.

Regarding the "rightly," Christianity has much to say. Pride is a great vice and humility (or meekness) a blessed virtue. But overall, the highest moral action is self-sacrificial service to the needs of others.[52]

As far as how humans know the above, it is through faithful, unquestioning acceptance of higher authority. This is essential, whether from the Bible directly or from other recognized authority.

This is core Christianity in a nutshell. In keeping it so brief, there is some oversimplification, but it captures the essence. And remarkably, on core belief, there is homogeneity of belief through an enormous diversity of Christian denominations and sects.[53]

Nonetheless, despite the homogeneity, differences of emphasis are evident. For the large Evangelical population these differences of emphasis are quite dramatic. This is the world of Christian fundamentalism.

FUNDAMENTALIST CHRISTIANITY

Tenets: Fundamentalist Christianity is largely Evangelical Christianity. Fundamentalism is sometimes considered a controversial term. Nevertheless, it is legitimate and useful.

Christian fundamentalism shares the core beliefs of all Christians, discussed earlier. But there are three pronounced differences of emphasis.

First, scripture, literally interpreted, is the sole source of knowledge and values. Second, the Christian must reject any separation of the sacred and the secular, whether in personal life or public. Third, there is a rejection of modernity among most fundamentalists.[54]

For the most part, these three areas of emphasis are *not* shared by mainline Christianity. Although a mainline Christian might be sympathetic to—or even share—one or more of them, it would tend to be the exception, rather than the rule.

By contrast, the typical fundamentalist will emphasize all *three* areas. As such, the practice of fundamentalist or Evangelical Christianity is easily seen as *extreme* Christianity.

Actually, however, its practice is more consistent Christianity. Its practice is more fully in line with Christian teaching. The concept "fundamental" is appropriate.

Development: Some historians view the evolution of evangelical Christianity in America as a series of pulsations that they call "Great Awakenings." This conceptual framework, though not universally embraced, is useful. Looking at the big picture, it is evident that religious fervor ebbed and flowed—retreated and revived—a number of times in America. And the periods of revival, or "awakening," reveal the decidedly fundamentalist nature of Evangelical Christianity.

EVANGELICAL CHRISTIANITY: EVOLUTION

Great Awakenings	Key Events	Responding To
First 1730's to 1800	Evangelicalism arrives in America from England	The aridity of Puritan Calvinism
Second 1790 to 1840	Evangelicalism reasserts itself, intensifies and grows	Secularism of American Enlightenment
Third 1850 to 1920	*The Fundamentals* (12 volumes) & WCFA (in 1919)	*Post Civil War modernism*
Fourth 1930 to 1980	Christian Right & Moral Majority Movements	Secular "evils" (abortion, gay rights, etc.)

The revivals were periods during which major changes occurred in the religious climate of the country. Forceful and colorful personalities—zealots—drove these changes, and in every case the changes were lasting ones, producing a cumulative effect on the later religious history of the country. There were four such epic periods, and each responded to perceived threat.[55]

Importance: It is important to grasp the role of Fundamentalist Christianity in American culture. First, it comprises a significant percentage of the American population. Surveys repeatedly confirm the 25% statistic, and that figure is referring to the percentage of the *entire* American population.

Second, this segment of American Christianity has penetrated deeply into the Republican Party. And third, it is also the segment of American Christianity advocating the view that America was founded as a Christian nation whose destiny is to be guided by Christian precepts.

Political Activism: By the late 20th and early 21st century, thousands of fundamentalist evangelical pastors plus millions of their flock became convinced that Christian duty compels political involvement. They consider themselves Republicans, the party of "traditional" values. The Christian Right, averse to modernity and secularity, largely controls the Republican Party platform in all states but the six in the Northeast and the District of Colombia.[56]

This did not happen overnight. It was during the fifty years of the fourth "Great Awakening" that Christian fundamentalism became entrenched, *deeply* entrenched, in American culture. During that period numerous fundamentalist alliances formed, similar to the World Christian Fundamentals Association (WCFA).

Large independent congregations formed as forerunners of the later mega churches. Bible colleges and institutes spread across the land.

Widespread use of print and electronic media techniques advanced the Christian cause and opposed school prayer prohibition, abortion, gay rights, and other aspects of modernity and secularity. There was large scale recruiting of fundamentalist Christians into politics as various Christian Right movements and initiatives became major forces.[57]

THE CHRISTIAN-NATION QUESTION

Religion and the Framers of America: The Founding Fathers often voiced religious belief. Religion was not unknown to them. That said, it is important to realize that many of them subscribed to Deism, a common religion among Enlightenment intellectuals.

In the Declaration of Independence, the expressions "Laws of Nature and of Nature's God" and the "Creator" are typical deist formulations. Other expressions are at the end of the Declaration, with references to the "Supreme Judge of the world" and "Divine Providence." But for the Deist, God was merely a disinterested spectator after creation—passive and impersonal—who then simply allowed the universe to unfold according to natural law.

The Deist concept of God is essentially different from the God of Christianity. The Christian Right's claim that the founders intended to establish a Christian nation does not have support in the Declaration of Independence.

Nor does it find support in the Constitution. There is no reference to God there, and its two references to religion are in the form of prohibitions. The First Amendment contains the famous "disestablishment" clause, and Article VI prohibits any kind of religious test for public office.[58]

A "Deistic Conspiracy": Historians tell us that a frequent charge from Christians in 1787 and 1788, the dates of the constitutional conventions and ratification proceedings, was that the Constitution "represented a deistic conspiracy to overthrow the Christian commonwealth." Many Christian thinkers were infuriated by the thoroughly secular nature of the Constitution, realizing its "godless" character.[59]

Despite this, today's Christian Right, would have us believe that the country was founded Christian and that the secularists have been undoing it ever since. Such rewriting of the facts has no support; on the contrary, it distorts history.[60] The *actual* fact is that religious forces have many times sought the "undoing" of the Constitution's godless nature with a "Christian amendment"—unsuccessfully so far.[61]

The Tyranny of State Religion: Many of the Founders were not Deists but Christians. Some were both. But predominantly they viewed religion as a private affair—in their words, a "matter of conscience."

The Founders knew their history well. At that time, as today, history stands as proof that to favor any one religion is to pave a sure path to tyranny.

Looking at the history of early America, we see that some of the most ardent opponents of state-sponsored religion were fervent Christians themselves. One of the most articulate was the famous Puritan minister, Roger Williams, the 1636 founder of Rhode Island.

Williams was a passionate advocate of Church-State separation.[62] He, like so many others after him, realized that to favor any one religion tyrannically violates the religious freedom of anyone *outside* that religion, including non-believers.

They likewise realized that to violate one right, in this case the right to freedom of conscience, establishes precedent that rights are *not* unalienable—which would gravely threaten *all* rights.[63]

A Vast Distortion: Where then does the notion stand that America's Founders were aiming to form a Christian nation? In short, it appears to be revisionism. It betrays an ignorance of who the Founders were and what they were about, namely, rights and freedom.

It distorts history. All indications are that the Founding Fathers agreed with the earlier Roger Williams that, if you violate freedom of conscience, or even compromise it, then it would be a mere matter of time before all rights and freedoms would be compromised and violated.

Kramnick and Moore, the scholars often cited in this chapter, are actually quite sympathetic to religion and regard it as a positive social force. But after exhaustively exploring the Christian-Nation issue from many angles, they conclude that it is not merely a distortion of history, but a *vast* distortion.[64]

ZEUS AND 21ST CENTURY AMERICA

Christian America: Despite the above, today's America might be viewed as a *de facto* Christian state, simply on the basis of demographics. After all, 75% of the American population pledges allegiance to Christianity, across an enormous diversity of denominations and sects and sub-sects.

More importantly, is that a full quarter of America's total population is *Evangelical* Christian. And Evangelical Christianity, defined by the three criteria identified above, is basically fundamentalist.

In addition, there are Christian fundamentalists from other sources. Hard statistics are difficult to come by, but the percentage of Christian Americans who are fundamentalist, surely a quarter, could well be upwards of a third of America's entire population.

In light of such considerations, it is easy to conclude that America, early in the 21st century, though not a *de jure* Christian state, is a *de facto* one.

A Rampant Religiosity: Religion is a real phenomenon. Directly or indirectly, it affects all Americans and renders America the most religious country in the developed world.[65] On the one hand, 21st century America is highly secular, and on the other, a rampant religiosity seems to pervade it.

It values science and technology; it pursues prosperity and material values. But it also engages in an enduring and sometimes torrid love affair with religion.

For most Americans, however, such "one-hand-other-hand" analysis is irrelevant because they deftly incorporate both "hands" into their lives. We will see this in the coming chapter.

As America's Enlightenment faded, Zeus reasserted himself. America's original Promethean spirit—intellectual defiance—faded. It met its demise. The way was opened for another mindset—and another spirit—gradually to fill the vacuum.

---

[41] Leonard Peikoff, *The Ominous Parallels, op. cit.,* p.115.

[42] Ibid., p. 105.

[43] An abundance of material is available on the Internet. Charles Pierce's 1878 essay "How to Make Our Ideas Clear" was the historical basis of Pragmatism. Pierce [1839-1914] coined the term.

William James [1842-1910] is another founder. His essay "What Pragmatism Means" sets forth Pragmatism's theory of truth.

John Dewey [1859-1952] is sometimes viewed as the one who made pragmatism respectable and is regarded as bringing it to its completion.

[44] For a brief history of pragmatism from the standpoint of its philosophic roots, especially the epistemologies of Kant and Hegel, see Leonard Peikoff, *op. cit.,* pp. 126-138. Dewey's view of thinking as a dis-ease is discussed on pp. 128-129.

For an analysis of pragmatism's impact on America's current culture, see Tara Smith, "The Menace of Pragmatism," *The Objective Standard,* Vol. 3, No. 3, Fall 2008, pp. 71-93, http://www.theobjectivestandard.com/issues/2008-fall/menace-of-pragmatism.asp, available as a PDF download.

[45] For an excellent source on the origin, role, and nature of religions throughout history, see intellectual historian John Ridpath's "Religion vs. Man," available as a 3 hour MP3 download through the Ayn Rand Institute eStore, https://estore.aynrand.org/search?q=Religion+vs.+Man.

[46] Of course, to be fully accurate, America's culture is Judeo-Christian because both traditions share a common world view, as set forth in the Old Testament. In addition, throughout American history, Jewish intellectuals have played a major role.

But the shorter and simpler term, Christian, is used throughout this work, for two reasons. First, the Christian population is vastly larger in number, but, more importantly, the political activism of religious fundamentalists, explored in this chapter, is primarily a Christian phenomenon.

---

[47] For the "Prosperity Gospel" see Cathleen Falsani, "The Worst Ideas of the Decade," *The Washington Post,* July 12, 2013, http://www.washingtonpost.com/wp-srv/special/opinions/outlook/worst-ideas/prosperity-gospel.html.

For "New Calvinism" see Josh Burek, "Christian faith: Calvinism is back," *The Christian Science Monitor,* March 27, 2010. http://www.csmonitor.com/USA/Society/2010/0327/Christian-faith-Calvinism-is-back.

[48] The enormous complexity of it all is quickly evident by a search on any of these groups. *Wikipedia The Free Encyclopedia* is usually a good starting point for some of the basics and for extensive references.

For Jimmy Carter, see Austin Cline, "Evangelical Christians and American Politics," http://atheism.about.com/b/2006/08/17/evangelical-christians-and-american-politics.htm. About.com Guide, August 17, 2006.

[49] See Jordan G. Teicher, "Why Is Vatican II So Important?," *NPR News,* October 10, 2012, http://www.npr.org/2012/10/10/162573716/why-is-vatican-ii-so-important.

[50] "Nondenominational Christianity," *Wikipedia The Free Encyclopedia,* last modified July 6, 2014, http://en.wikipedia.org/wiki/Nondenominational_Christianity.

[51] Nancy Gibbs, "Apocalypse Now," *Time Magazine,* http://www.time.com/time/magazine/article/0,9171,1002759,00.html, July 1, 2002, p. 45.

[52] Regarding the humble, the meek, and the poor in spirit, this tenet is most clearly stated in the "Sermon on the Mount." In the Bible's King James Version, *Matthew* 5:3 states, "Blessed are the poor in spirit: for theirs is the kingdom of heaven." Two verses later *Matthew* 5:5 reads, "Blessed are the meek: for they shall inherit the earth." Meekness thus blesses the Christian practitioner in both heaven and on earth.

Regarding self-sacrificial service to others, it will be discussed at length in the next chapter.

[53] Calvinism tends to be an exception. See again "New Calvinism," several notes above.

[54] There is likely to be disagreement on modernism. But some heavy hitters would be Darwinian evolution, doctor assisted suicide, gender alteration, new reproductive technologies.

[55] See Rice University's William Martin, *With God on Our Side: The Rise of the Religious Right in America,* revised trade paperback edition (New York: Broadway Books, 2005).

The 1996 original hardcover edition by Broadway Books was the companion volume to the PBS television documentary series by the same name.

Martin reserves the term "Great Awakenings" to the 1st and 2nd periods in my table, but not the 3rd and 4th.

[56] *Ibid.,* Introduction, pp. 1-23, captures many aspects of this political activism, which the balance of the book extensively elaborates.

For a concise summary of the Religious Right's penetration into the Republican Party, see also William Martin, "Three Paths To Eden: Christian, Islamic, and Jewish Fundamentalisms," pp. 9-11, (The James A. Baker III Institute For Public Policy: Rice University, May 2006). The web address is too lengthy to cite here, but the title is easily accessible on the Internet, and the PDF format readily made readable using "PDFLite" freeware.

[57] In "Three Paths To Eden" (previous note), Martin argues for the legitimacy of the "fundamentalist" label and refers at times to Christianity's "Religious Right" as a "morphed fundamentalism." The three tenets that I take to be of greatest significance in "fundamentalism" are adapted from a longer characterization of fundamentalism by Martin in his "Paths to Eden" essay. The three that I identify are readily perceivable in evangelical Christianity, and can be seen as a "morphing" of Martin's lengthier, but always lucid, characterization of fundamentalism.

---

[58] The text of the famous "Disestablishment" clause has already been quoted. Article VI reads, "[N]o religious Test shall ever be required as a Qualification to any Office or public Trust under the United States."

[59] Isaac Kramnick and R. Laurence Moore, *The Godless Constitution*, revised ed., with a new chapter (New York: W. W. Norton, 2005), p. 34.

[60] *Ibid.*, pp. 11-25. These pages, comprising the first chapter of *The Godless Constitution*, are devoted to the issue. Also see Joseph Kellard, "In Reason We Trust," *Capitalism Magazine,* June 10, 1998, pp. 4-5, http://capitalismmagazine.com/1998/06/in-reason-we-trust/.

[61] *Ibid.*, pp. 144-148.

[62] *Ibid.*, pp. 46-66. It is a tribute to the stature and influence of Roger Williams that Kramnick and Moore devote all of their chapter three to him.

[63] One famous document articulating this very point is James Madison's 1785 "Memorial and Remonstrance Against Religious Assessments." http://religiousfreedom.lib.virginia.edu/sacred/madison_m&r_1785.html.

[64] Kramnick and Moore, *op. cit.*, p. 149. Their entire book can be read as an exploration, either directly or indirectly, of the Christian-Nation issue.

Chapter 7 in particular, pp. 131-149, deals with the many attempts through the years, both successful and unsuccessful, to inject Christianity into American culture, with special attention to the often attempted "Christian amendment."

[65] Matthew Hay Brown, "U.S. is most religious in industrialized world," *Baltimore Sun*, December 16, 2009. http://weblogs.baltimoresun.com/news/faith/2009/12/united_states_is_most_religiou.html.

IV. The Post-Enlightenment Mindset

America's original spirit is not the spirit of today's America. In essence, the original spirit was an implacable intellectual defiance in the face of tyrannical authority.

Intellectual, in this context, means based on principles and reason. As such, it was a product of the Enlightenment. It was *reason-based* defiance.

A country's "spirit" is a metaphor for the dominant emotional tone of its individual men and women, but especially of the "movers and shakers." For late 18th century America, the movers and shakers were the Founding Fathers, intellectuals who were also men of action.

But as the Enlightenment faded, their defiance met its demise. A new mindset took over and persists to this day, as well as the new spirit it cultivated. This new mindset is the Post-Enlightenment mindset.

Today's Post-Enlightenment Mindset

America's Post-Enlightenment mindset consists of two tenets. The first is that man is inherently weak, even depraved; the second is that self-sacrificial service to the need of others is the highest form of moral behavior. They are two of Christianity's core beliefs.

Scope: The scope of this mindset is great. It is automatically embraced by the 75% of the American population that pledges allegiance to Christianity, across that enormous diversity of denominations and sects and sub-sects named in the last chapter.

Vital to realize, however, is that the mindset is also shared by the remaining 25% of America's population as well. That is, non-Christians, agnostics, and atheists also believe in a) the alleged weakness and depravity of human nature, and b) that self-sacrificial service is the greatest virtue. Exceptions are relatively few.

Explanatory Power: A mindset is more of an implicit outlook than an explicitly held position. It is a fixed mental attitude or state of mind.

In the case of America's Post-Enlightenment mindset, people for the most part are not aware that they hold its two tenets. But, together, the tenets possess great explanatory power in American culture. They permeate it, as we shall see.

Origin and Codification

Despite its connection to Christianity, the Post-Enlightenment mindset did not originate with Christianity. Rather, both its tenets originated in prehistory, with the earliest appearance of *Homo sapiens*.

Human Weakness and Depravity: Regarding this alleged aspect of human nature, there was the constant need for early humans to confront the raw dominance of the physically stronger. Reason as an alternative to force was yet to be explicitly identified, and savagery of man toward man was not uncommon.

This continued even after mankind realized that reason was an alternative to force. Terror could arrive at any moment—not only from earthquake, flood, or wild creature—but also, most disturbing of all, from other humans.

In the face of this, it would have been natural to conclude that human beings are naturally evil and rapacious. Even today, it is a ready conclusion when force, not reason, is made the rule. Tragically, this is the case throughout much of the world.

Early religions reinforced that conclusion. Creation myths sought to explain where we came from, how we should live, and why evil exists.

World views often tended to divide existence into two realms, a spiritual one of perfection and light, and the physical one of this earth, filled with dark imperfection and outright evil. This dualistic metaphysics not only sought to delimit and explain evil, it also sought to mitigate its horror by offering a better place, a supernatural realm where evil does not hold sway and where man's depravity—that phenomenon of the imperfect physical realm—has no place.

Service as the Greatest Virtue: Again, a look at prehistory points to the origin of *this* tenet as well. Prehistoric peoples realized the need to pool resources and to gain strength through numbers. They faced an intensely hostile environment and knew they had to depend on one another to survive. Faced with that reality, and again, prior to an explicit recognition of reason, it was easy to surrender the individual to the group, such as by forcibly pooling resources and effort.

Codification: At first, oral traditions reflected these two tenets. Later, as writing developed, written scriptures codified them.

Of great influence in the West is the *Old Testament* account of man's original fall in the Garden of Eden. This "original sin" is Christianity's explanation of man's innate depravity. Most if not all early religions have parallel accounts.[66]

Of course, the path to the other tenet is a direct one. Weak and depraved natures must not be left free to pursue their own interests; this can only lead to evil. The antidote: make it a moral imperative in a holy book or scripture that man must put the needs of others before his own. Once scripture dictates this, compliance is more easily enforced and deviations are more readily punished—by God and by society.

Written scriptures, throughout the world, have long codified the two tenets of the Post-Enlightenment mindset. Formulations vary, and some are clearer than others, but, overall, one can spot the tenets.[67]

REINFORCEMENT

Everyday Usage: The tenets of the Post-Enlightenment mindset produce many clichés. "Man cannot be trusted to be honest; left to his own devices, a businessman will victimize his employees, cut corners, defraud customers, and unscrupulously savage his competitors." Or, "unfettered capitalism is dog-eat-dog; government regulation is needed to reign in man's animal impulses."

These familiar statements, and many others like them, directly proceed from the dogma that man is innately weak and inclined to evil. Each statement is a dogmatism or bromide spun from that primary dogma.

Again, "There are far too many needy people; therefore it is only right and fair that government entitlement programs meet those needs." Or, "We need to help those who are less fortunate; therefore it is only right that the government heavily tax the rich."

Each of these familiar pronouncements, as well as many others, rests on the dogma that service to the need of others is the highest form of moral behavior. Again, each assertion or sentiment functions as a dogmatism spun from that primary dogma.

Used by Authorities: Authority figures regularly advance the Post-Enlightenment mindset. In the first few minutes of his 2009 commencement address at Notre Dame, President Barak Obama clearly attributed "violence and want and strife," and all the other "cruelties" of human nature, to "what those of us in the Christian tradition understand to be rooted in original sin."[68]

On the day before, First Lady Michelle Obama gave a commencement address at the University of California in Merced and declared, "Service is the rent we pay for living ... it is the true measure, the only measure of our success."[69]

The two most visible authority figures of the time could not have been clearer in their enunciation of the tenets of the Post-Enlightenment mindset. Nor did anyone think twice.

The media reported these statements as if they were entirely commonplace, which of course they were. Both are cultural bromides in Post-Enlightenment America.

Barak Obama campaigned for the presidency on the need to serve and sacrifice to others. Both before and after election, he regularly cited passages from the Bible to justify a program or initiative.

Repeatedly, he underscored to the religious Right—the Republicans—that *he*, not them, was the consistent Christian. That is, he was saying that he on the Evangelical Left understands what Christianity requires better than those of the Evangelical Right.[70]

The exhortation to serve is standard fare in commencement addresses. Republican Governor, Bob McDonnell of Virginia, at the University of Richmond's 2012 commencement, declared, "Serving others is the highest calling for a person in our society .... Be great and serve."

Public figures in other venues as well, regularly—and inadvertently—promote the Post-Enlightenment mindset. In 2011, republican presidential hopeful, Governor Rick Perry, held an evangelical prayer rally in Houston for the economy. During it he prayed, "Lord .... You are our only hope and we stand before you ... in gratitude for your blessings, and humility for our sins." He followed with, "our heart breaks for America ... and ... we cry out for your forgiveness."

Tenet one of the Post-Enlightenment mindset is at work here. Perry is seeking "forgiveness" for man's weakness and depravity.[71]

The fact that one would hold such a view of human nature and yet pursue wealth and prosperity, as Perry does, is not uncommon for evangelical Christians. For them, this is what God wants. Their unstated premise would simply be that God's grace makes it possible to pursue one's own interests without fear of victimizing others in the process.[72]

The Changed American Spirit

The Enlightenment Concept of Human Nature: The Enlightenment held a decidedly optimistic and benign view of human nature. For the typical Enlightenment thinker, human nature is lawful and perfectible.

In 1799, Jefferson wrote that "I believe ... man's mind is perfectible to a degree of which we cannot as yet form any conception." We need to "preserve the freedom of the human mind," he continued, "...for as long as we may think as we will and speak as we think, the condition of man will proceed in improvement."[73]

For the Enlightenment thinker, the torch of reason was carried high. Mind was seen as a ruling force. "Fix reason firmly in her seat," Jefferson urged his nephew Peter Carr, "and call to her tribunal every fact, every opinion. Question with boldness even the existence of a God; because, if there is one, he must more approve of the homage of reason, than that of blindfolded fear."

To Benjamin Rush, Jefferson declared in 1800, "I have sworn upon the altar of God, eternal hostility against every form of tyranny over the mind of man."[74]

For the Enlightenment thinker, the doctrine of innate weakness and depravity was alien. He was well familiar with its long history, as any educated person would be, but to regard it as innate was seen as mistaken.

Weakness and depravity *were* recognized, but not as innate to man. For Enlightenment man, the power of the reasoning mind enables him to resist and rise above any such tendencies.

The Enlightenment on Service: The typical Enlightenment thinker saw service to others as a good. One can readily find passages in Thomas Jefferson, Thomas Paine, and Benjamin Franklin to illustrate this.

But it was not the stress. It was not the highest virtue. The Enlightenment intellectual would sooner grant that stature to personal development, in all its manifestations.

This was especially the case in the area of the intellect. Personal development had priority over all else. It expressed itself time and again in exhortations to self-sufficiency, self-reliance, and like virtues. It is vividly clear in that letter of Jefferson to his nephew Peter Carr.

Contrasting Mindsets: The difference is dramatic between the Enlightenment and Post-Enlightenment mindsets. On the Enlightenment mindset, man is perfectible through reason and self-development.

By contrast, the Post-Enlightenment mindset sees man as inherently weak, even depraved. Such a creature is not to be measured by what he makes of himself, but by how well he serves others. As mentioned earlier, this last is his "only measure of ... success."

Contrasting Spirits: Because each mindset is dramatically different in content, each of them creates a climate in which the prevailing *spirit* is different as well.

In Enlightenment America, the reasoning mind made intellectual defiance possible, specifically defiance in the face of tyrannical authority. Again, *intellectual* here means based on reason and principles, such as the principle of unalienable rights.

But, as the reasoning mind was gradually replaced by a conviction of man's weakness and depravity, the game changed. Instead of intellectual defiance, man now all-too-easily looks to a higher authority for strength, for guidance—and, as Rick Perry strikingly illustrated—for forgiveness.

The evidence is compelling that compliance to authority has supplanted defiance.

Entrenchment: Americans carry the Post-Enlightenment mindset like a lens that has been surgically implanted without their knowledge. And once implanted, it colors how they view a) human nature (weak and depraved) and b) how they believe life is best to be lived (in service to others).

Taken together, the two tenets of the Post-Enlightenment mindset set Americans up for higher authority. It disarms them in advance.

Americans—whether "man in the street" or intellectual—might feel inclined to defy an authority's call for sacrifice. But the authority simply needs to remind them of what they have already accepted, to exploit that fact. President Obama, as indicated earlier, is quite skilled at this.

The Post-Enlightenment mindset is largely entrenched in America—an unchallenged part of her intellectual infrastructure. And, early now in the 21st century, many measures are in place to keep it entrenched—measures to ensure that Prometheus's spirit—the defiance of tyrannical authority personified by America's Founders—does not again reassert itself in America on a significant scale.

They are the same measures that the wrathful Zeus took with Prometheus in order to squelch *his* defiant spirit. Chains.

---

[66] *Genesis* 2:16 to 3:24. The fact that the beginning of the first book of the Old Testament has this account attests to its foundational importance in Christianity.

[67] *World Scripture, A Comparative Anthology of Sacred Texts,* Dr. Andrew Wilson, Editor (International Religious Foundation, 1991). On the degradation of human nature: http://www.unification.net/ws/theme056.htm and on serving others: http://www.unification.net/ws/theme138.htm .

[68] See "Obama Notre Dame Speech," *The New York Times,* http://www.nytimes.com/2009/05/17/us/politics/17text-obama.html?pagewanted=all. May 17, 2009.

---

[69] See "Michelle Obama's Commencement Address," http://www.nytimes.com/2009/05/16/us/politics/16text-michelle.html?pagewanted=all&_r=0. *The New York Times*, May 16, 2009

[70] For abundant evidence of Barak Obama's Evangelical Left activism, see philosopher Craig Biddle's "The Creed of Sacrifice vs. The Land of Liberty," *The Objective Standard*, Vol. 4, No. 3, Fall 2009, http://www.theobjectivestandard.com/issues/fall-2009/creed-of-sacrifice-vs-land-of-liberty/.

[71] Re. Governor McDonnell's commencement address, see Jeremy Slaton, "McDonnell urges UR graduates to make a difference, serve others," *Richmond Times Dispatch*, updated January 18, 2013. http://www2.timesdispatch.com/news/local-news/2012/may/07/tdmet01-mcdonnell-urges-ur-graduates-to-make-a-dif-ar-1895737/.

Re. Governor Perry's rally, see Manny Fernandez and Daniel Cadis, "Prayer Rally Draws Thousands in Houston," *The Caucus*, The Politics and Government Blog of *The New York Times*, August 6, 2011, http://thecaucus.blogs.nytimes.com/2011/08/06/prayer-rally-draws-thousands-in-houston/

[72] Aman Bathea, "Texas Gov. Perry became a millionaire while serving in office," *The Miami Herald*, August 29, 2011, http://www.miamiherald.com/2011/08/29/2379942/texas-gov-perry-became-a-millionaire.html.

[73] "Thomas Jefferson: On Science and the Perfectibility of Man," excerpt from June 18, 1799 letter to William Green Mumford, *Encyclopedia Britannica Profiles*, The American Presidency,

http://www.britannica.com/presidents/article-9116908. Source: "A Tribute to Philip May Hamer on the Completion of Ten Years as Executive Director, the National Historical Publications Commission," New York, December 29, 1960.

---

[74] Thomas Jefferson, letter to his nephew, Peter Carr, from Paris, August 10, 1787, Merrill D. Peterson, ed., *Thomas Jefferson: Writings* (New York: Library of America, 1994), pp. 900-906, http://www.stephenjaygould.org/ctrl/jefferson_carr.html.

For the Letter to Rush, http://www.let.rug.nl/usa/presidents/thomas-jefferson/letters-of-thomas-jefferson/jefl134.php .

V. Chains – The Wrath of Zeus

In Aeschylus's great drama, Prometheus incurs the wrath of Zeus by brazen defiance. He steals the god's fire—the fire of reason and thought—and gives it to mankind in order to lift it from darkness.

Symbolically, America's Founders did the same. They stole Enlightenment philosophy—lit with the *same* fire of reason and thought—and developed it to form a new and unique republic. Again, Zeus was defied.

First, after casting off the tyranny of English rule, the Founders had the effrontery to form a government whose function is to serve the individual. No longer is government to be man's lord and master. Thus Zeus, in his government form, had been effectively stripped of power over mankind.

Second, America's Founders again symbolically defied Zeus in his alternate form as Christian God. They ratified a godless constitution and made god strictly a matter of private conscience. No longer was any god to be publically favored. Again, Zeus had been effectively stripped of power.

Never before in human history had such brazen acts of defiance been seen.

But, just as Zeus retaliates in Aeschylus's myth, chaining Prometheus for thousands of years, so too does today's modern Zeus. Symbolically, Zeus still exists. He has taken form in two incarnations of great authority: government and god. And in each of them, we can see the same method of retaliation at work—chains. Indeed, Zeus lives on—and thrives.

Government Chains: History & Features

Coercive regulation is force initiated by government edict to control the actions of individuals who are otherwise voluntarily dealing with one another. They are not violating the rights of others or threatening to do so.

Yet the government sees fit to intervene, effectively chaining what it deems to be bad behavior. The phenomenon is endemic and costly; the annual price tag of complying with federal regulation is upwards of $2 trillion.[75]

Background: The regulatory state did not happen overnight but has a well-documented and, in this Internet age, readily-accessed history. In 1876 the Supreme Court decision in *Munn v. Illinois* established the precedent that any property "clothed with a public interest" (that is any property used to conduct business) is subject to government regulation and control.

This major landmark set the stage for even greater landmarks: the Interstate Commerce Act of 1887 and the Sherman Antitrust Act of 1890. These were soon followed in 1913 by the creation of the Federal Reserve and the inauguration of the income tax via the Sixteenth Amendment.[76]

Sherman marked the end of what was, until then, largely unfettered capitalism in America. It also marked the start of the Progressive Era, which ran from the 1890's to the 1920's.

There were many other programs, but even from the few cited, it is evident that by the early 20th century government intervention had become firmly established. Then intervention grew throughout the century, as did the income tax, the vehicle that made possible the financing of it.

Regulation Today: Now, in the 21st century, government authority exerts itself in all sectors of the economy and touches the personal lives of every citizen.

The financial industry in particular is the most regulated sector of the American economy. "Of all the claims made about the financial crisis [of 2008]" two authors write, "none is more preposterous than that the financial industry was a bastion of freedom."[77]

Though privately owned on paper, the "Fed" has always been under government control. The Federal Reserve has long been the central organ by which government controls the American financial system. To claim that that it is an independent entity is, again, preposterous.[78]

Large bodies of coercive regulation regularly appear now in the 21st century. Notable among them are the 2003 Sarbanes-Oxley Act (or "SOX") and the 2010 Affordable Care Act (or "Obamacare").

SOX was in response to massive accounting fraud by the Enron Corporation. It led to wide government regulation of the accounting standards of U.S. big business. This is necessary, regulators insist, to keep businesses honest.[79]

Obamacare was in response to the health care crisis, astronomical medical costs, and the existence of Americans without health care coverage.[80]

At the state and local levels, too, Americans face ever-increasing oversight into private affairs. The *Nanny State* is the term coined for this phenomenon, and the fact that it appears to have gone wild receives much attention.[81]

New York City attempted to ban sugary soft drinks larger than sixteen ounces in order to help address the nation's obesity "epidemic." Though the initial attempt was unsuccessful, it is a colorful example and significant in that it was even tried.

Government regulations, both large scale (SOX and Obamacare) and modest (sugary soft drinks), are a great reality in American life. They cut across all sectors of the economy and drill down into all areas of private life.

Most Americans simply take them for granted. Like death and taxes, they are *just there*. And, whether federal, state, or local, government regulations exhibit common features.

The Initiation of Force: Whether a regulation is large or small in scope, the government is initiating force against private individuals or groups who are engaged in activities that do not infringe or threaten the rights of others. Clearly the government is looking to prohibit, compel, or control behavior that hitherto was free.

Coerced Compliance: The individuals targeted by coercive regulation have no choice but to obey or else face the penalties incurred anytime laws are violated. That is, regulation is backed by the coercive power of government to force compliance. Noncompliance is not an option, unless one wishes to undergo prosecution or fine or imprisonment—or all three.

Precedence: Once the government has its foot in the door, fully opening the door is easy. As already cited, *Munn v. Illinois* was a major instance of this in 1876.

Smoking bans in the 20th century were a result of the same dynamic. Regulations on cigarette smoking started with prohibitions on certain types of advertising and eventually led to prohibitions on *where* the government will allow people to smoke.

Implicit Premises: All coercive regulation rests upon implicit premises, usually unstated. In the large sugary drinks case, two are discernable: consumers are innately weak, and business owners are innately depraved for pandering to that weakness.

Observe that each of them are instances of tenet one of the Post-Enlightenment mindset. The Enlightenment viewpoint that reason enables an individual to counter tendencies to weakness and depravity, should that individual have developed them, is effectively preempted.

Chains on Behavior: The metaphor is exact. Coercive regulation controls behavior. Some regulations control by *prohibiting* or chaining *down* behavior, such as prohibiting the offering and consumption of sugary soft drinks larger than sixteen ounces.

Other regulations control by *compelling* certain behavior, as if leading the regulated party by chains around the neck. In each case, chains are at work coercively molding behavior.

Advocates of government regulation are explicit on this point. "We need to pass strong regulations," declares a Nobel laureate in economics, "embodying norms of good behavior, and appoint good regulators to enforce them."[82]

The Rational Faculty Denied: Regulations negate the free choice, judgment, and intelligence of the regulated parties—both providers and consumers. This of course is always a side effect of initiated force.

The fact that regulations invariably do this in the name of some authority's pre-conceived notion of "good behavior" does not alter the reality that coercion is involved.

CHAINS OF CHRISTIANITY

With three quarters of America's population pledging allegiance to Christianity, America is clearly the most religious developed country. Religion is pervasive and the need for it is rarely questioned.

Quite the contrary, most people regard it as a necessity, as the source of morality, and as a palliative to man's alleged innate weakness and depravity.

Thus they commonly regard religion as a positive and healing force in American life.

They are not likely to think of Christianity in terms of chains. And so this needs to be demonstrated, for the chains are real but less than obvious.

Christianity's Chains of Darkness: Essentially, Christianity requires the unquestioning acceptance of its doctrines on the basis of higher authority. It replaces reason—the faculty by which humans evaluate evidence in order to gain knowledge of reality—with unquestioning faith.

Consider the following. Christians accept without question the existence of a supernatural dimension in which a supernatural being exists. Christians accept without question that human nature is sullied with innate weakness, even depravity, because mankind sought to partake of the "Tree of Knowledge" in the "Garden of Eden." Christians accept without question that there is an eternal life for which this "earthly" one is a mere preparation. Christians accept without question that Jesus was the incarnation of God on earth.

All such beliefs are accepted at an early age. This is expected—effectively *demanded*—of any child born into a Christian family. And the beliefs get reinforced throughout life—by scripture, catechism, minister and teacher.

Thus do they become a part of the typical Christian's world view, never to be questioned.[83] Indeed, for most of them, the fact that someone might entertain an alternate world view has scant reality. For the typical Christian, that fact, effectively, is inconceivable.

Quantifying the chains: Three out of four Americans—Christians—accept without question that the destiny of individuals and nations is guided by a supreme being residing in another, higher dimension.[84] One out of three Americans—Christians—accept without question, that the Bible is the literal word of God.[85]

Because of their Christian faith, three times more Americans accept without question the Virgin Birth of Jesus than Americans believing in Darwinian evolution.[86]

Three out of four Americans—Christians—accept without question the existence of angels, and four out of five unquestioningly accept the existence of miracles.

Christian faith has nearly six out of ten Americans convinced that "the bloody predictions in the Book of Revelation—which involve the massacre of everyone who has not accepted Jesus as the Messiah—will come true."[87]

Large groups of the Christian faithful accept without question that the Bible, not the will of the people, should shape U.S. law.[88]

The Virtue of Obedience: Christian intellectuals are uncomfortable with the charge that their religion abandons reason. This is understandable since there is a tradition of scholarship based on respect for reason in mainline Christianity.

Nonetheless, apart from certain theologians and a small proportion of lay intellectuals, Christians generally do not concern themselves with *Apologetics*, a systematic, logical defense of Christianity.

On the contrary, the essential element for the Christian—a *virtue* even—is unquestioning obedience to higher authority. This is how one earns eternal happiness. "Except ye be converted, and become as little children," said Jesus, "ye shall not enter into the kingdom of heaven."[89]

Reason Abandoned: Whether we look at fundamentalist or mainline Christianity, minds, young and old, are taught, and become accustomed—not to reason and think independently—but to embrace some authority higher than reason, whether it be Bible, revelation, teacher or preacher.

Even sense perception is unnecessary. A famous exchange between Jesus and the doubting apostle, Thomas, makes that clear. "[B]lessed are they that have not seen," Jesus tells him in *John* 20:29, "and yet have believed."

Young minds are especially malleable, and vulnerable. A Jesuit educator is credited with the boast, "Give me the child till the age of seven, and I will show you the man"— concisely capturing the lasting power of early indoctrination.[90]

The Wrath of Zeus

America's original spirit of defiance—*reason-based* defiance—is now largely supplanted by compliance. Once again, the twin tyrannies of unlimited government and dogmatic religion dominate.

Chains are the tool of forcing compliance—those of coercive regulation in the case of one and of Christian unreason in the case of the other. By means of chains, the wrath of the symbolic Zeus, in both his modern incarnations, expresses itself in today's America.

Willing Compliance Expected—and Given: The idea that Americans remain defiant in the face of Zeus's wrath is largely a myth, if one means *principled, reason-based* defiance. The defiance of our Founding Fathers was based on the principle of individual rights. But that principle has long been abandoned in America, usually inadvertently, even by those who would oppose government coercion.[91] In general, principled defiance is difficult to find in an age of unreason.

Though forced compliance is an unavoidable aspect of any government regulation, discussed earlier, forced compliance often evolves to *willing* compliance. All Americans, for instance, are willing members of various *fiscal constituencies*. That is, Americans are willing beneficiaries of various entitlement programs driven by coercive government regulation.

Other Americans—businessmen—willingly form *crony* relationships with government regulators. They form these alliances in order to use the government's coercive power against their competitors. Many businesses readily accept, or seek *corporate welfare*.

***Tea Party "Defiance"*:** The hugely significant Tea Party phenomenon of the early 21st century is based on defiance to government chains.

Tea Party defiance, however, is clearly more emotional than intellectual. It is largely based on America's perennial pro-freedom spirit. They are effective advocates for smaller government and less government coercion.

But many of them also advocate for coercive programs. In large numbers, they too have inadvertently abandoned the principle of individual rights, as originally conceived by America's Founders. Thus their defiance tends *not* to be intellectual.[92]

Willing Compliance of the Adult Christian: For children born into Christian households, compliance in the face of religious authority is effectively forced. The Jesuit boast suggests a form of brainwashing.

But, except for a small minority, religious indoctrination is more a form of strong conditioning, not brainwashing. Christian adults do not lose their faculty of volition. As adults, they develop the psychological maturity to question childhood indoctrination.

Typically, however, they find it easier simply to go along with what is so familiar to them. Statistics suggest that for most adult Christians, compliance to religious authority, at least on basic belief, remains a reality.

This compliance is a combination of choice—to stay within their comfort zone, on one hand—and continued unthinking acceptance, on the other. And so, when questioned, they declare themselves *Christian*, thereby joining the huge American population, three quarters of the total, that does the same.

The Self-Perpetuating Nature of Zeus's Chains: Chains of Christian unreason and chains of government coercion both perpetuate themselves.

As explained earlier, Christian chains are chains of darkness, or *un*reason. Thus they strongly tend to perpetuate themselves for they have compromised the tool by which one escapes *any* intellectual darkness. That tool is the faculty of reason.

Chains of government coercion inevitably perpetuate themselves as well. By their very nature, they render Americans *willingly* compliant. At that point Americans *want* to see those chains continue. And so *they* get perpetuated too.

***

Whether compliance to chains is passive, forced, or willing, America is largely—not totally, but *largely*—wound in chains. And defiance—real, fierce, principled, *reason based*—has largely vanished.

In pronounced contrast, Prometheus, still in chains at the end of Aeschylus's great drama, remains defiant. He lets out a mighty roar: "Behold me. I am wronged."[93] He did *not* stand before Zeus "in humility for [his] sins." He did *not* "cry out for forgiveness." Governor Rick Perry of Texas did *both*—as he presumed to speak for all America during his 2011 evangelical prayer rally for the U.S. economy. Though Perry was speaking as an evangelical Christian, mainline Christians did not take exception to his exhortation, nor did secular intellectuals. This is an eloquent indication of what America has become.

Despite his fierce defiance, however, Aeschylus's Prometheus still needed help from another mythical figure in order to escape his chains. That was Heracles. America, too, needs help, and in actual fact, an American Heracles figure *did* appear—in the 20th century.

---

[75] *Ten Thousand Commandments: An Annual Snapshot of the Federal Regulatory State*, (Competitive Enterprise Institute: updated annually), http://cei.org/10KC. *Code of Federal Regulations* (U.S. Government Printing Office: updated annually), http://www.gpo.gov/fdsys/browse/collectionCfr.action?collectionCode=CFR.

[76] Michael Dahlen traces this history in "The Rise of American Big Government: A Brief History of How We Got Here," *The Objective Standard*, Vol. 4, No. 3, Fall 2009, with 101 endnotes. Available as a PDF download. http://www.theobjectivestandard.com/issues/2009-fall/rise-of-american-big-government.asp.

Regarding the 1876 Munn v. Illinois case, Dahlen excerpts the chilling words of Chief Justice Morrison Waite, as follows: "When ... one devotes his property to a use in which the public has an interest, he, in effect, grants to the public an interest in that use, and must submit to be controlled by the public for the common good"

[77] Yaron Brook and Don Watkins, *Free Market Revolution*, (New York: Palgrave Macmillan, 2012), p. 53. On the same page, the authors list eight regulatory bodies governing the U.S. financial system at the national level alone.

---

[78] See George Reisman, *Capitalism: A Treatise on Economics*, (Laguna Hills, California: TJS Books, 1998), p. 965, note 92, where he makes clear why the Fed functions as a political entity, not an independent entity.

[79] "Sarbanes-Oxley Act," *Wikipedia, The Free Encyclopedia*, http://en.wikipedia.org/wiki/Sarbanes–Oxley_Act, last modified July 14, 2014.

[80] For a concise listing of the key provisions, see "Affordable Health Care for America Act," *Wikipedia, The Free Encyclopedia*, http://en.wikipedia.org/wiki/Affordable_Health_Care_for_America_Act, last modified June 27, 2014.

[81] For the origin of this descriptive term, see *Wikipedia, The Free Encyclopedia*, http://en.wikipedia.org/wiki/Nanny_state.

[82] Joseph E. Stiglitz, "In No One We Trust," http://opinionator.blogs.nytimes.com/2013/12/21/in-no-one-we-trust/?_r=0,a December 21, 2013 excerpt from *The Great Divide*, a series on inequality, in the *New York Times*.

[83] Undoubtedly, for some young believers, there is curiosity about the beliefs on which they have been raised. The subject of God is fascinating, because the underlying philosophical issues are fascinating.

There is the issue of God's existence, with its fascinating arguments, pro and con. There is the issue of faith versus reason, with the fascinating counter arguments each position needs to face.

A comprehensive single source for these and many other issues is George H. Smith, *Atheism: The Case Against God*, First Edition, 1979, (Amherst, NY: Prometheus Books, 1989).

[84] Susan Jacoby, *The Age of American Unreason,* (Vintage: New York, 2009), p. 201. Jacoby no doubt has in mind the often-confirmed statistic, that three-quarters of the American population declares itself Christian.

[85] *Ibid.,* p. 188.

[86] *Ibid.,* p. 206.

---

[87] *Ibid.,* p. 18. For the statistic relating to belief in the *Book of Revelation*, Jacoby cites Nancy Gibbs, "Apocalypse Now," *Time*, July 1, 2002.

[88] *Ibid.,* pp. 190-191, citing a 2006 survey by the Pew Forum which found that this was true of 60% of white, evangelical Christians, 16% of white mainline Protestants, 23% of Catholics, and 53 to 44% of black Protestants.

[89] King James Bible, *Book of Matthew*, 18.3.

[90] There are various versions of this well known boast, all of them basically saying the same thing. See http://uk.answers.yahoo.com/question/index?qid=20070825015743AAtbNey.

[91] The modern abandonment of the original concept of rights will be discussed in the next chapter.

[92] For the inconsistencies of the Tea Party, see Ari Armstrong, "To Help Save America, Tea Partiers Must Fully Embrace Individual Rights," *The Objective Standard Blog,* http://www.theobjectivestandard.com/2010/08/to-help-save-america-tea-partiers-must-fully-embrace-individual-rights/, August 20, 2010.

[93] Edith Hamilton, *Three Greek Plays*, (New York: W. W. Norton & Company, 1937), p. 143.

VI. HERACLES

Early in the second half of the 20th century, a notable change occurred in American television. A young journalist, along with a few like-minded colleagues, decided that the time had come to attack the television interview, a programming staple, in a new way. His name was Mike Wallace.

His idea was to replace the "pablum" (his word) of the interviews of the time with in-depth, in-your-face, probing into the thinking, the causes, and the controversy of colorful characters of the time. Extensive prior research was to ensure accuracy and relevance. If the provocateur selected for interview had abused a sacred cow or two along the way, well, that was a good thing.

The new approach was a hit. It began as *Night-Beat* in 1956 and soon became *The Mike Wallace Interview* which ran from 1957 to 1960. On February 25, 1959, Wallace's guest was the hugely controversial Ayn Rand.[94]

It was her first appearance on national television, and it would be followed by many more public appearances prior to her death over two decades later. But no subsequent interview matched this particular face-off.

Rand had just turned 54 and had completed her masterwork, *Atlas Shrugged*, two years before. If radical, colorful individuals made good TV—and this was Wallace's quest—he was not disappointed in Rand.

My purpose in this chapter is to continue the leitmotif of the Prometheus myth and show how Ayn Rand can be seen as an American Heracles figure. I intend to demonstrate that Rand, by her philosophy generally and her championship of reason specifically, has provided the means for cutting through the chains of Zeus in both his modern incarnations. These are his twin incarnations as government and as God, as I delineated them in previous chapters.

In doing so, I intend to present Ayn Rand's thinking as an unleashing into the world—on a scale not seen since America's founding—of a promethean-like defiance to authority. Rand gives meaning to the term, "radical intellectual."

Rand the Person

Early Life: Ayn Rand was born in 1905 in St. Petersburg, Russia, now Leningrad. From an early age, she knew that she would be a writer; at 16, she enrolled in Petrograd State University where she focused on history and philosophy. She sought to understand man's development through the study of history (her major) and to objectively define her values through the study of philosophy.

She lived through the Revolution, but escaped Russia in 1926 on a visitor's visa, knowing she would never return. When she arrived in a fog-enshrouded New York harbor on February 19th, she was, as biographer Jeff Britting reports, accompanied by "mental outlines of seventeen novels, screenplays, and plays."[95]

America: Ayn Rand was a passionate woman, but about three things above all: Frank O'Connor (her husband of more than 50 years), America as the country of individual freedom and opportunity, and her writing.

As she got to know America first hand, she was dismayed to discover the extent to which American freedom had been eroded by the 1920's. This dismay, coupled with the fact that she had first-hand experience of the Soviet dictatorship and, thus, of how far a country could sink, throws light on much of her writing. As it matured, along with her command of English, her writing reflected her matured thinking as well.

By the time of her bestselling 1943 novel, *The Fountainhead,* her philosophy was largely formed; by the time of her 1957 *Atlas Shrugged*, she had articulated it in all its essentials. *This* is the Rand that Mike Wallace introduces to the television world in 1959. She is more than ready for prime time.

Rand on the Vital Role of Reason

As Mike Wallace so skillfully brings out, Ayn Rand's ideas are incendiary. Indeed, this is exactly the kind of television he loves. In one person, he has a flaming champion of unfettered capitalism as well as an unabashed champion of self-interest or, in her words, *rational egoism*. But most startling for many viewers is that Rand is an avowed atheist (though not a militant one).

The Fundamentality of Reason: Rand was clearly intransigent on these issues, but she did not consider them the most fundamental. Several years later, she makes that clear: "I am not primarily an advocate of capitalism," she declares, "but of egoism, and I am not primarily an advocate of egoism, but of reason. If one recognizes the supremacy of reason and applies it consistently, all the rest follows."[96]

For anyone seeking to grasp Rand in her role as a modern-day Heracles figure, the importance of this statement cannot be overemphasized.

In three millennia of Western civilization, human reason rules only twice. The first occurrence is in the Greece of antiquity; the second is the Age of the Enlightenment, the seeds of which are first sown, in earnest, during the Renaissance. I touch upon these two ages in previous chapters.

Rand's Question: Aeschylus, Aristotle, Albertus, Aquinas, and many Enlightenment intellectuals, including America's Founders, revere reason and, especially in the cases of Aristotle and Aquinas, how it functions. But none of these giants explicitly ask *why* it is that reason deserves to be revered.

It would seem that they took it as self-evident. A not uncommon notion is that reason enables man, somehow, to partake of the divine. But for Rand, reason is a distinctly human (not divine) faculty *and* deserves to be revered.

Reverence for human reason is a theme of Ayn Rand's work, indeed, of her entire life. This is clear in three works I believe to be among her greatest achievements. Each has a separate header, below, to indicate the discipline in which she is working.

REASON IN RAND'S ETHICS

In February 1961, nearly 35 years to the day after her arrival in a fog-enshrouded New York harbor, Ayn Rand delivers a paper at a University of Wisconsin symposium on ethics. At that point, she has fully articulated a revolutionary morality of rational egoism and has named her philosophy, *Objectivism*. The paper she delivers at the symposium is titled "The Objectivist Ethics."[97]

Rand's Approach: Rand's approach to ethics starts with two fundamental questions: "What are values? Why does man need them?" That is, she starts with the specialized area known as *metaethics* which deals with the underlying issues of a given ethics.[98]

In answering these questions, Rand makes a number of key identifications, among them the facts that only the concept of life makes the concept of value possible (and needed) and that for any living being, life is therefore, of necessity, the ultimate value.[99]

But, unlike all other living organisms, man does not automatically know what values he needs to pursue in order to survive and thrive. He needs to discover them and then produce them himself. Reason—along with thinking, its process—is the means by which he does this, the *only* means.

All other life forms have automatic knowledge of what they need to pursue in order to survive; by contrast, man has *no* automatic knowledge.[100]

Rand's Objectivity: It is from such starting points that Ayn Rand provides an objective basis for her ethics of rational egoism. She argues that man's rational nature dictates his survival needs. Of necessity then, reason is man's cardinal value and rationality his cardinal virtue. And further, Rand argues for "man's life as the *standard* of value—and *his own life* as the ethical *purpose*."[101]

She advances an ethics based on the principle that human life does not require sacrifice, where she defines sacrifice as the surrender of a higher value to a lower one or to a non-value. Hers is an ethics of rational selfishness. According to it, man neither sacrifices himself to others, nor others to himself.

Just as life is an "end in itself," she points out, "so every living human being is an end in himself, not the means to the ends or the welfare of others." Hers is an ethics in which *"the achievement of his own happiness is man's highest moral purpose."*

Hers is a moral code in which "productive work is the central purpose of a rational man's life, the central value that integrates and determines the hierarchy of all his other values."

In the political realm, her moral code promotes the basic social principle that "no man may initiate the use of physical force against others." And it promotes laissez-faire capitalism as the only social system under which the implementation of that principle is fully possible.[102]

A Scientific Method: Throughout this seminal essay, Rand clearly emphasizes man the thinker, uniquely surviving and thriving by means of reason and thought. She is not simply stating it, she is demonstrating it, by observation of man, by contrasting observations of other life forms, and then reasoning on the basis thereof.

Essentially, Rand is using the scientific method to define an *objective* ethics. She is defining an ethical system whose source is not religion, not society, and not subjective feelings. Rather it has an objective source, namely, the facts of reality.

For the first time, ethics is the function of that which nature requires for man to survive and thrive.[103] In short, the source is man's nature as man.

Does Ayn Rand demonstrate that the faculty of reason deserves to be revered? For anyone who takes the time to understand the reasoning behind her ethics (the above is a mere sketch), the answer will be, yes. For anyone who grasps her identifications of human life as the ultimate value, of what is needed to achieve and sustain it, and then of what is needed to flourish, the answer, again, will be, yes.[104]

Reason in Rand's Fiction

As indicated, Ayn Rand makes clear in her ethics that it is only through reason that man survives and thrives. Her fictional masterwork, *Atlas Shrugged,* underscores and dramatizes this.[105]

It is vast in scope and, now, many years after initial publication, it annually sells in the hundreds of thousands. Its theme, as stated by Rand, is "the role of the mind in man's existence."

Reason versus Coercion: In *Atlas Shrugged*, Rand presents man fully exercising his rational faculty to think, create, and produce through voluntary trade with like-minded producers.

Also dramatized is the man who evades thinking, who sabotages his rational faculty, and who uses coercion rather than voluntary trade in dealing with his fellow man. Most vivid of this type are the many government-business cronies who populate the novel. These are the individuals to whom readers of *Atlas Shrugged* frequently relate, so vivid are the parallels to the business world of today's America.

The Force of Reason: Reason as the ruling force in man's existence is a theme that Rand clearly and compellingly illustrates in a way only possible through the stylized reality of romantic fiction.

Rational men flourish when they deal with other rational men, voluntarily trading value for value. Irrational men, such as the multitude of today's government-business cronies, use force to expropriate the wealth of the producer. It might not be right away, but ultimately these types perish in their own corruption, as the novel dramatizes.

Does Ayn Rand demonstrate that the faculty of reason deserves to be revered? For anyone who has read *Atlas Shrugged* and has grasped its parallels to today's heroes and villains, the answer will be, yes.

Reason in Rand's Epistemology

Objectivist Epistemology: "The Objectivist Ethics" and *Atlas Shrugged* — touched on in the above—are two of the three works that are among Ayn Rand's greatest achievements. The third work in the trio is her *Introduction to Objectivist Epistemology*.

This work followed "The Objectivist Ethics" by five years, appearing initially as a set of eight essays in Rand's journal, *The Objectivist*, from July 1966 to February 1967. Just as *Atlas Shrugged* is Rand's masterwork in the field of fiction, *Introduction to Objectivist Epistemology* is her masterwork in the field of philosophy.[106]

The Problem of Universals: In this work, Rand sets out to solve the central problem of philosophy, that of concepts—known historically as the "problem of universals." As Rand puts it, "since man's knowledge is gained and held in conceptual form, the validity of man's knowledge depends on the validity of concepts."

In the forward to *Introduction to Objectivist Epistemology*, she clearly sets forth the issues. She points out that, while concepts are abstractions, "everything that man perceives is particular, concrete."

This raises such questions as what is the "relationship between abstractions and concretes" and "to what precisely do concepts refer in reality?" Rand briefly indicates that, historically, there are different schools of thought. While some thinkers propose that concepts actually exist in reality in some form, others propose that concepts are merely inventions of man's mind. Still others argue that concepts are arbitrary constructs or loose approximations that cannot claim to represent knowledge.[107]

The complexity of the problem of universals is great, and its importance cannot be overstated. Rand recognizes that "in the light of [the above] 'solutions,' the problem might appear to be esoteric." But then she reminds us "that the fate of human societies, of knowledge, of science, of progress and of every human life, depends on it. What is at stake here is the cognitive efficacy of man's mind."[108] Of course, such statements are completely consistent with the advocacy of reason in her ethics.

Ayn Rand's theory of concepts avoids the pitfalls of earlier schools of thought. Instead, she provides original, unique, and lucid answers.

As in all her work, she is exercising reason, defined by her as the faculty which identifies and integrates the material provided by man's senses. That which rules throughout her writing is observation—keen observation—and then applying reason to it by a process of thinking—again, the essence of the scientific method.

Rand on Kant: Rand points to Immanuel Kant as the great subverter of human reason. His is the philosophy for which she reserves the greatest contempt. Kant's destructive power, she repeatedly points out during her life, is great and his influence on subsequent thought is enormous.[109] *Introduction to Objectivist Epistemology* is Rand's full response and antidote to Kant.

Does Rand demonstrate that the faculty of reason deserves to be revered? To anyone who has studied and grasped Ayn Rand's epistemology (the above is a bare outline), the answer will be, yes.

She champions human reason in the face of those who abandon reason. She elucidates reason for those seeking to understand it. She defends reason against those seeking to undercut and subvert it.

Rand on the Chains of Christian Unreason

Christianity Expects Docility: As noted in chapter five, Christianity requires the unquestioning acceptance of its doctrines on the basis of higher authority, whether by scripture, catechism, preacher, or teacher.

Docile, childlike compliance is expected. The Bible states it quite clearly with, "Except ye be converted, and become as little children, ye shall not enter into the kingdom of heaven."[110] Christianity thus chains the believer's mind with chains of unreason and makes the wearing of those chains a virtue.

Rand, by contrast, cuts through such chains and makes reason a cardinal value and rationality a cardinal virtue. In her ethics, there is no place for unquestioning acceptance—of anything—not if one's goal is to live a flourishing life on this earth as a rational and independent human being.

Volition in Rand: Regarding the Post-Enlightenment mindset, Ayn Rand demonstrates the fundamental error of considering weakness and depravity as essential aspects of human nature.

For her, the essential aspect of human nature, essential because it explains and makes possible the greatest number of other aspects of man, is his mind.[111] Yes, many men *are* weak and many men *are* depraved, but these are not inherent in their nature. On the contrary, man possesses the faculty of reason which enables him to resist and overcome (with time) weakness and depravity, should he have allowed such tendencies to form.

But its exercise is volitional. Yes, weakness and depravity exist, but they are acquired by choice, and, over time, can surely become habitual ways of functioning. They can also be induced, or at least incentivized, by other men. But these facts do not make weakness and depravity innate to man.[112]

Christians, as well as non-Christians, commonly hold that man has a natural "tendency" to evil. But, as Rand points out, this conflicts with the general Christian belief in free will (Calvinism excepted). As she puts it, "A free will saddled with a tendency is like a game with loaded dice .... If the tendency is of his choice, he cannot possess it at birth; if it is not of his choice, his will is not free."[113] (Ayn Rand would say the same of the doctrine of *grace*, the widespread Christian notion that the faithful receive help in the form of God's grace to counter their innate tendency to weakness and depravity.)

Rejection of Altruism: Regarding the second tenet of the Post-Enlightenment mindset, that altruism, or self-sacrificial service to others, is man's greatest virtue, Ayn Rand demonstrates why rationality is the highest virtue and *not* altruistic service to others.

Throughout her life's work, she demonstrates that rationality is the source of all human achievement and all that is good in human life. She demonstrates that rationality is the great enabler of all the other virtues, such as honesty, justice, independence, and integrity. Her ethics is rich in content.

By contrast, service to others, as a moral imperative, is an ethics devoid of content. As Rand points out, the "beneficiary of moral values is merely a preliminary or introductory issue in the field of morality." It is "not a substitute for morality nor a criterion of moral value, as altruism has made it."[114]

Does Rand sunder the chains of Christian unreason? For the Christian believer, the answer would be, no. Chains of unreason tend to be self-perpetuating. To abandon reason, is to abandon the primary means of escaping *any* chains.

What Rand *has* done, however, is provide the means of sundering the chains of Christian unreason. There are honest Christians, good people, who do not realize the betrayal of reason their religion requires. Should they ever wish to explore that betrayal, and address it, the means are provided—in the pro-reason philosophy of Ayn Rand.

RAND ON THE REGULATORY CHAINS OF GOVERNMENT

Capitalism: Ayn Rand is famous as an advocate of capitalism. She defines it as "a social system based on the recognition of individual rights, including property rights, in which all property is privately owned."[115]

For Rand, capitalism means pure, unregulated, laissez-faire capitalism. In short, she advocates capitalism without chains.

A Mixed Economy is Not Capitalism: Rand identifies America's system as—*not* capitalism—but a mixed economy, an unstable mixture of private ownership and government control. This volatile blend of free enterprise and socialism, continually trends to greater stagnation and ever-tightening chains of coercive regulation. Eventually and necessarily, she stresses, it leads to some form of socialism.[116]

Post Atlas Shrugged: After *Atlas Shrugged,* Rand devoted herself to non-fiction writing. She founded a number of journals, she wrote essays, she gave lectures, and she made television appearances. It was two and a half decades of prolific output prior to her death in 1982.

I want briefly to discuss four works that stand among Ayn Rand's clearest for featuring her as a modern-day Heracles figure severing *government* chains. They are: "Man's Rights," "The Nature of Government," "Notes on the History of American Free Enterprise," and "America's Persecuted Minority: Big Business."[117]

"MAN'S RIGHTS" [118]

A Nation of Rights: During her lifetime, Ayn Rand often observes that America is the first nation to be founded on the principle of individual rights where by a "right' she means *"a moral principle defining and sanctioning a man's freedom of action in a social context."*[119]

Because the Founders base their new republic on this concept, America is the first country in human history to make society, including government, subservient to the individual and to moral law.

The Founders strictly limit government to one function, and one function only—the protection of individual rights. "The most profoundly revolutionary achievement of the United States of America," Rand states, "was *the subordination of society to moral law."*[120]

Society, of course, includes the government. For the first time in history, rights protected the individual from the government.

Rights Are Grounded in Observable Fact: Rand strongly differs from the Founders, however, on the origin of rights. Where they see rights as self-evident, God-given principles, she is the first to develop the deeper philosophy that provides the foundation for rights.

Contrary to the Founders, she demonstrates that rights are grounded in observable fact. Ayn Rand's thinking is a revolutionary development in the theory of rights. It is encapsulated in this seminal essay.

Today's "Group" Rights: It is vital to note Rand's insistence that a "right" is a concept that pertains only to freedom of individual action. That is, it applies to "freedom from physical compulsion, coercion, or interference by other men."[121]

In the second half of "Man's Rights," Rand provides abundant evidence that today's America has virtually abandoned the original conception of rights. As she demonstrates, America has taken the original meaning of rights (to action) and reversed it to mean the right to objects and services. This, she emphasizes, necessarily negates rights. It necessarily entails violating the rights of the men who must be forced to provide those products and services. Who does the forcing? Government does. Rights—reinterpreted to apply to objects and services—tacitly gives government that power. Group rights, Ayn Rand repeatedly argues during her life, are a total corruption of the original concept of rights.

"The Nature of Government" [122]

Strong Government Indispensable: Despite her advocacy of pure capitalism, Rand regards a strong, properly-defined government as an indispensable precondition if men are to live together in peace and harmony. In fact, she holds this view—not *despite* her advocacy of pure capitalism—but *because* of it.

"A government," on Rand's definition, "is an institution that holds the exclusive power to *enforce* certain rules of social conduct in a given geographical area."[123]

As she explains it, a proper government bars physical force from social relationships. That is, a proper government makes reason the exclusive way that men have to deal with one another. This means "discussion, persuasion and voluntary, un-coerced agreement."[124]

Objectively Controlled Force: But, as Rand observes in this essay, men can violate the rights of others. They do so deliberately or inadvertently. They do so individually or as members of a group. Because this can happen, rights necessitate the right to self-defense. And this is where government comes in.

In Rand's formulation, if "physical force is to be barred from social relationships, men need an institution charged with the task of protecting their rights under an *objective* code of rules." And this, she continues, "is the task of a government—of a *proper* government—its *basic* task, its only moral justification and the reason why men do need a government."

In short, a government, in Ayn Rand's luminous prose, "is the means of placing the retaliatory use of physical force under objective control—i.e., under objectively defined laws."[125]

Related Issues: In "The Nature of Government" Rand develops a number of key related issues. There is the issue of the scope of government. (It needs to embrace three areas: police, military, and courts.) There is the issue of whether government is evil by nature and, thus, whether anarchy is the ideal social system. (It emphatically is *not*, contends Rand.) There is the issue of the role of the constitution in a properly-formed government. (The constitution's purpose is to limit the government, not the private individual, Rand stresses.)[126]

Finally, Rand deals with the issue of how government can become man's deadliest enemy. (It does so by turning its coercive power against the men that that power is supposed to protect, thereby abrogating their rights.)[127] We see this happening in America (chapter 5) and throughout the world.

"NOTES ON THE HISTORY OF AMERICAN FREE ENTERPRISE"[128]

Successful Railroads vs Failed Roads: This essay focuses on the history of the American railroad industry. Here is Rand as historian first and then as penetrating interpreter of history. The following are a few highlights of what she uncovers.

Foremost is the notion that railroads would have been impossible without government financial help. As Rand reveals, this is historically false. In fact, the railroads that solicited and received government help were the ones that failed; history proves that the most successful roads were built without government help.[129]

The failed roads carry a history of corruption, bribery, and outright dishonesty. All these were made possible because government intervention creates a system in which dishonesty is inherent.

Rand presents case after case to substantiate this indictment, along with sources. All are part of the historical record.[130]

The Evidence of the Great Northern: J. J. Hill's Great Northern Railroad successfully opened the entire Northwestern part of the continent to development without seeking or taking a penny of government help.[131]

The "evils popularly ascribed to big industrialists," Rand points out, "were not the result of an unregulated industry, the conventional view, but of government power over industry." In defiance of common belief, and contrary to what detractors of free enterprise perennially claim, the "villain in the picture was not the businessman, but the legislator, not free enterprise, but government controls."[132]

"AMERICA'S PERSECUTED MINORITY: BIG BUSINESS" [133]

Antitrust Law Persecutes: Throughout her life, Ayn Rand insists that antitrust (where "trust" translates to "coercive monopoly" in the mind of any "trust-buster") is the arena in which government coercion is at its most vicious in America. Indeed, her theme in this piece is that antitrust is nothing short of rank persecution.

Strong charges, in support of which Rand marshals an enormous amount of evidence. Since her evidence is so readily accessible, I will simply touch briefly on some of the highlights and allow the reader to pursue the details, as well as the evidence.

Antitrust law is notoriously nonobjective, to the point where, as Rand states in an earlier article, antitrust law gives the government "the power to prosecute and convict any business concern in the country any time it chooses."[134]

At every turn, the government denies to big business basic rights thought to be possessed by all Americans. It requires the businessman to prove his innocence if accused of unfair competition. This, of course, stands in blatant violation of the presumption-of-innocence principle on which America's court system is based. Yet, it is an unavoidable result since, under antitrust laws, "a man becomes a criminal from the moment he goes into business, no matter what he does."[135]

Guilt is Unavoidable: If a bureaucrat judges that his prices are too high, the businessman is guilty of "intent to monopolize." If his prices are lower than those of his competitors, he is guilty of "unfair competition" or "restraint of trade." If a businessman's prices are the same, the trust-buster can prosecute him for "collusion" or "conspiracy."

The laws are adaptable and interpretation is always on a case by case basis. But, once the trust-buster decides to flex his muscles, the hapless businessman cannot *not* be found guilty of some violation of antitrust law.

And the threat of such persecution always exists, for antitrust law is retroactive or ex post facto law, "a basic evil," Rand reminds us, "rejected by Anglo-Saxon jurisprudence."[136]

The Evidence: Rand provides ample evidence for each of these outrages. Real-life, flesh-and-blood figures abound in her address.

Bureaucrats and judges are quoted, with their words standing as clear evidence that minority rights do not exist for the businessman. Consistent with the Post-Enlightenment mindset, belief in the businessman's alleged depravity is unquestioned.

Rand examines five well known antitrust court cases that stand as historical evidence. Of these, it is the *General Electric* case of 1961 that she views as the most egregious. As she puts it, this case is the "ultimate climax which makes the rest of that sordid record seem insignificant ..." Reading this essay, or listening to the address, it is difficult not to come to the same conclusion, especially today. Even now, more than half a century later, Americans regularly witness case after case repeating the same syndrome of persecution.[137]

The Scapegoat: One might ask at this point, how such persecution could exist in America, the "land of the free." This is another chilling portion of Rand's address, and, in it, she uncovers a number of related issues.

Among them is the fact that, throughout history, persecuted minorities serve as scapegoats for the evil of others. In America, she demonstrates, businessmen are scapegoats for "the evils of the bureaucrats."[138]

AYN RAND AS HERACLES

Looking back at the four works just discussed, can it be said that Ayn Rand has sundered the regulatory chains of government unreason? As with the chains of Christian unreason, the answer is, no. Again however, Rand has provided the *means* of sundering those chains.

"Man's Rights" and "The Nature of Government," closely related, provide the essential infrastructure or political philosophy needed if America is to have free enterprise without chains. A proper understanding of the nature of rights and of government is far from a reality today, early now in the 21st century. Rather, Rand's political philosophy stands as an ideal. But without first the ideal, the elimination of chains will not become a reality.

It bears noting here that Rand's radical political philosophy, on a number of points, stands in contrast to libertarianism.[139]

"Notes on the History of American Free Enterprise" and "America's Persecuted Minority: Big Business" are also closely related. Together, they deal with the dishonesty, coercion, and corruption inherent in any system in which government intervenes in the economy. Together, they demonstrate that, perversely, it has always been the businessman who gets blamed for the sins of the bureaucrat. In short, both works cut through the lies and distortions which have always been used to justify chaining free enterprise.

Chapter five, above, demonstrated that chains, whether from God or from government, necessarily coerce an individual's mind with an authority higher than his faculty of reason. Reason then, is the only antidote to such coercion, and, historically, reason found its greatest champion in an American immigrant-intellectual.

The world knows her as Ayn Rand.

We have it in our power ...

America today is largely bound by chains—not completely—but largely. Many are the intellectuals working to keep those chains in place. Many are the people who seek to counter them, but unwittingly support them instead. Many are the forces that seek to break government chains only to replace them with others. But chains *can* be broken.

Thomas Paine said it best. "We have it in our power," he proclaimed in the Appendix to his 1776 *Common Sense*, "to begin the world over again."

Today's America needs to begin over again, and that will take a return to the spirit underlying America's founding. That is, it will take a return to reason-based defiance.

Ayn Rand's philosophy stands as a towering monument to such defiance—the greatest such monument in human history.

---

[94] http://www.youtube.com/watch?v=1ooKsv_SX4Y. (Search Youtube, if this link becomes inactive.)

[95] Jeff Britting, *Ayn Rand*, (New York: Overlook Duckworth, 2004), pp. 20, 22, 31. This definitive biography is lavish in its use of photographs from the Ayn Rand archives.

[96] "Brief Summary" in the final edition of Rand's journal, *The Objectivist,* Vol. 10, September 1971, p. 1089.

---

[97] The date was February 9, 1961, and the symposium was "Ethics in Our Time."

The address was later published as the lead essay in Ayn Rand, *The Virtue of Selfishness*, Signet paperback (New York: 1964), a collection of essays, with introduction.

The introduction is especially relevant to the lead essay, "The Objectivist Ethics."

[98] "Objectivist Ethics," *The Virtue of Selfishness,* Signet paperback (New York: 1964), p. 15.

[99] *Ibid.*, pp. 16-17.

[100] *Ibid.*, pp. 18-19.

[101] *Ibid.*, pp. 19-25.

[102] *Ibid.*, pp. 25, 27, 31-33.

[103] *Ibid.*, pp. 33-34.

[104] Tragically, many environmentalists look on human life as unnatural and intrinsically evil—a sign of the depravity of the age in which we live.

[105] Original hardcover edition, Dutton, (New York: Penguin Books, 1957).

[106] Published as a Mentor paperback, (New York: New American Library, 1979). The page references here are to the Meridian expanded second edition, co-edited by Harry Binswanger and Leonard Peikoff, (New York: The Penguin Group, 1990).

Also available as a Kindle book.

[107] *Introduction to Objectivist Epistemology*, p. 2.

[108] *Ibid.*, p. 3.

---

[109] For a cogent statement of her estimate of Kant and his influence, see Ayn Rand, "Faith and Force: The Destroyers of the Modern World," in *Philosophy: Who Needs It,* (New York: Bobbs-Merrill, 1982), pp. 77-79.

[110] King James Bible, Book of *Matthew*, 18.3.

[111] For Rand's explanation of what make a characteristic "essential," see *Introduction to Objectivist Epistemology*, chapter 5, "Definitions," especially pp. 45-46.

[112] Rand identifies the volitional nature of human consciousness in "The Objectivist Ethics," p. 20.

For a full explication, see Leonard Peikoff, *Objectivism: The Philosophy of Ayn Rand,* (New York: Penguin Books, 1991), pp. 55-62.

For the theory's validation, see pp. 55, 69-72.

[113] Ayn Rand, *For the New Intellectual*, (New York: Signet paperback edition, 1961), p. 137.

[114] *The Virtue of Selfishness*, (Signet paperback edition, 1964), Introduction page x.

[115] Ayn Rand, *Capitalism: The Unknown Ideal*, (New York: Signet paperback edition, 1967), p. 19.

All below references are to this paperback edition.

[116] Rand discusses the mixed economy at length in "The New Fascism: Rule by Consensus," *Capitalism: The Unknown Ideal.* See especially pp. 206-207 for the nature of the mixture.

And see pp. 202-203, where Rand points to fascism as a form of dishonest socialism, allowing private ownership but with government control. This is the essence of America's mixed economy.

Also on this subject is Rand's "The Fascist New Frontier," originally an address to The Ford Hall Forum, Boston, December 16, 1962. Now available as an MP3 download at the Ayn Rand Institute eStore.

---

[117] Each of the four works is contained in her 1966 *Capitalism: The Unknown Ideal.*

"America's Persecuted Minority: Big Business" is available as an MP3 download from the Ayn Rand Institute eStore.

"Man's Rights" and "The Nature of Government" are downloadable at no cost from The Ayn Rand Institute, http://ari.aynrand.org/issues/government-and-business/individual-rights/Mans-Rights#filter-bar .

[118] First published in *The Objectivist Newsletter*, Vol. 2, No. 4, April 1963. Later published in *The Virtue of Selfishness*, and *Capitalism: The Unknown Ideal.*

In *The Virtue of Selfishness,* the closely related 1963 essay, "Collectivized Rights," also appears, pp. 101-106.

[119] *Capitalism: The Unknown Ideal*, p. 321.

[120] *Ibid.*

[121] *Ibid.* p. 322. See also Craig Biddle, "Ayn Rand's Theory of Rights: The Moral Foundation of a Free Society," *The Objective Standard*, Vol. 6, No. 3, Fall 2011, Available as a PDF or as a free MP3 download, http://www.theobjectivestandard.com/issues/2011-fall/ayn-rand-theory-rights.asp.

[122] First published in *The Objectivist Newsletter*, Vol. 2, No. 12, December 1963. Later published in *The Virtue of Selfishness*, and *Capitalism: The Unknown Ideal.*

[123] *Capitalism: The Unknown Ideal*, p. 329.

[124] *Ibid.*, p. 330.

[125] *Ibid.*, p. 331.

[126] *Ibid.*, pp. 334, 336. Regarding the relation of the constitution to the individual citizen, Jefferson's view was the same. In the eighth of his Kentucky

Resolutions of 1798, he refers to the Constitution as chaining the government official from mischief. "In questions of powers," he states, "let no more be heard of confidence in man, but bind him down from mischief by the chains of the Constitution." See http://www.constitution.org/cons/kent1798.htm.

[127] *Capitalism: the Unknown Ideal*, p. 336.

[128] First published as a 1959 pamphlet, Nathaniel Branden Institute, New York, and later in *Capitalism: The Unknown Ideal*.

[129] *Capitalism: The Unknown Ideal*, pp. 102-103.

[130] *Ibid.*, pp. 104-105.

[131] *Ibid.*, p. 105. See also Talbot Manvel, "James J. Hill and the Great Northern Railroad," *The Objective Standard*, Vol. 6, No. 1, Spring 2011, pp. 89-102, PDF or MP3 available. http://www.theobjectivestandard.com/issues/2011-spring/james-hill-great-northern-railroad.asp.

[132] *Capitalism: The Unknown Ideal,* p. 102.

[133] Lecture given at The Ford Hall Forum, Boston, on December 17, 1961, and at Columbia University on February 15, 1962. Published by Nathaniel Branden Institute, New York, 1962, and later in *Capitalism: The Unknown Ideal.*

[134] Ayn Rand, "Antitrust: the Rule of Unreason," *The Voice of Reason*, (New York: Meridian, 1989), p. 258. First published in *The Objectivist Newsletter*, Vol. 1 No. 2, February, 1962, p. 8.

[135] *Capitalism: The Unknown Ideal,* p. 49.

[136] *Ibid.*, pp. 49-50.

[137] *Ibid.*, pp. 58-61.

---

[138] *Ibid.*, pp. 45-48. A prime illustration of this is the charge that a free market will lead to coercive monopolies. Rand often stresses that coercive monopolies require government intervention in the economy.

The historical record is clear, as she often pointed out, that coercive monopolies are not possible under full capitalism.

See also Nathaniel Branden, "Common Fallacies About Capitalism," *Capitalism: The Unknown Ideal*, pp. 72-77.

[139] See Craig Biddle, "Libertarianism vs. Radical Capitalism," *The Objective Standard*, Vol. 8, No. 4, Winter 2013-14, http://www.theobjectivestandard.com/issues/2013-winter/libertarianism-vs-radical-capitalism.asp.

Biddle clearly summarizes the contrasts and why they are vital to any defense of capitalism. Toward the end of his article, however, he makes a significant point. He points out that, provided there is no concession to the libertarian view that philosophy is unnecessary for the defense of liberty, "engaging with libertarians can be profoundly good."

VII. The Second American Enlightenment

America's history cannot be understood apart from a simple reality. America started life and then flourished during her first century and a half as a uniquely-designed republic in which men, ruled by reason, were largely free to go where their vision took them.

Today's reality is something different. *America, early now in the 21st century, is largely taken by an age of unreason, in which the rule is coercion.*

Prior chapters examined each reality. Chapter one, *Prometheus in America*, dealt with the role of reason in the founding of the new Enlightenment nation. Chapter two, *Reason Unbound*, examined the role of reason in her titanic growth. Chapter three, *Zeus in America*, explained why, despite her reason-based start, supernatural forces were able to reassert themselves so successfully in America. Chapter four, *The Post-Enlightenment Mindset*, dissected the age-old, anti-reason view of human nature that reasserted itself with the fading of the Enlightenment. Chapter five, *Chains: the Wrath of Zeus*, made clear how Zeus's two modern reincarnations—regulatory government and Christian God—chain human reason. Chapter six, *Heracles*, featured Ayn Rand, the 20th century philosopher-novelist who cut through those chains and unleashed reason on Earth once again.

This seventh and final chapter will project what is now possible: a Second American Enlightenment or Second Age of Reason. Together with chapter six, it makes good the promise in the subtitle of this book, namely, the rise, demise, and *recovery* of America's original spirit.

The Banning of Initiated Coercion

Reason versus Unreason: Intellectual history is overwhelmingly dominated by ages of unreason, punctuated with relatively brief periods of reason, like exclamation points. When reason predominates, man is free to think, to define his own destiny, and to criticize and defy tyrannical authority.

The vastly longer periods of unreason stand in stark contrast. In them, tyrannical authority disarms man by negating his rational faculty. Then it readily brings about compliance to *its* dictates. And as discussed earlier, much of that compliance eventually becomes *willing* compliance. Today's America is largely consumed by such an age. Once again, she is consumed by an age of *un*reason.[140]

An Invitation: So prevalent has coercion, or the threat of it become and so often veiled under a patina of civility, that many Americans today fail to appreciate how coerced they are. Many others accept that coercion in willing compliance.

As a result, Americans, generally, have scant motivation for imagining a social system in which force has been banned. That is, they have scant motivation for imagining a social system in which reason—the faculty that functions on observation, logic, and persuasion—has supplanted force as the culture's main driver.

This final chapter sets the imagination loose. In the coming pages, we enter a future America. We enter the age of America's Second Enlightenment. Sit back, and simply enjoy the excursion. Bear in mind that most of what follows once existed in an earlier America. This is the world of America's Second Age of Reason. It is now in full bloom.

An Unchained Social System: As we enter this world, the most visible and dramatic change in day-to-day existence is a social system in which government oversight does not exist. As we scan America's economy, gone are the innumerable coercive government regulations and gone the multitude of alphabet agencies that administered them. Gone is the Federal Reserve, the apparatus by which the government historically controlled the nation's financial system in its entirety.

The behavior police, looking to "enforce strong regulations embodying norms of good behavior" (chapter five), were out of work long ago. Individual judgment now rules, provided no one's rights are violated or threatened by force. People are free to make mistakes, to victimize themselves—to *misbehave*. It is now recognized that higher authority, whether god or government, has no business trying to force *good* behavior. Rational persuasion has replaced physical force or the threat of it. In essence, society is profoundly at peace.

The authority of reason is the only authority. Those who choose to follow paths of weakness and depravity—paths of *un*reason—do not fare well. The system of the past is now gone. That system not only permitted those paths to exist, but it positively paved them with gold.

To be sure, there exist those who exhibit human weakness and depravity. Individuals are free to develop such tendencies. Under *any* system, they have that choice and *should* have that choice, again, short of violating or threatening to violate the rights of others.

But now such people, if their chosen path is to live off the back of others, find themselves living in a social system unsympathetic to that path; entitlement programs have been phased out. Or, if their chosen path is somehow to violate the rights of others, they find themselves faced with a legal system implacable in its defense of individual rights.

Evils Eliminated: The resultant changes have been sweeping. Swept away is the ability of the politician to create vast fiscal constituencies (the entitlement-holder classes). Swept away is the ability of the bureaucrat to initiate and spawn crony relationships with business. Swept away are the government's perennial attempts to stimulate the economy. Special treatment, favoritism, and corporate welfare are gone, along with the evils they spawn.

Conversely, swept away is the ability of those in the private sector—banker, industrialist, scientist, educator—to seek a crony relationship with a government regulatory or funding agency. All this is preempted now that the public sector, the government, is constitutionally prohibited from intervening in the private sector. No longer can the public sector subsidize, license, franchise any part of the private sector.

Throughout history, the greatest specimens of human depravity have not been criminals. Rather they have been found in positions of authority. They have been kings, they have been emperors, they have been dictators, they have been popes. Above all, they have been governments that, in the absence of constitutional prohibitions to the contrary, had the power to initiate coercive force against their citizens.

Even in democracies, "government service" was a misnomer; it actually meant power over the individual citizen. It was an open invitation for the corrupt bureaucrat to choose weakness and depravity. It was also an open invitation for power-seekers to pursue government employment in the first place.

With rare exceptions, such evils were rife in all civilizations throughout history. All such depravity is now swept away in America. America in her Second Enlightenment is the first country ever to have so completely done so, by *constitutionally* limiting government to the sole function of protecting individual rights.[141]

Swept away is the endemic pressure group warfare throughout the economy, both private and public, each group looking to employ government force against its "enemies," that is, other pressure groups. Such a corrosive phenomenon is now in the distant past. The government has been stripped of the economic power—that is, the purse strings—that invited pressure groups and made them inevitable.

Weakness and depravity, whether in the private sector or public, are no longer viable options. It has nothing to do with whether humans are naturally good or evil. (As volitional beings, they can choose to become either.) Rather it is the existence of a system that prohibits anyone, anywhere, from initiating force against other humans. It is a system intransigently, punishingly opposed to any attempts to do so.

Now in America's Second Age of Reason, reason completely rules in place of coercion. Government is limited solely to the protection of individual rights and voluntary, coercion-free trade. With government out of the private sector, the pervasive and corrupting influence of government force initiated against private citizens (chapter five) is no more.

No longer can economic power become political power, or political power become economic power. Those powers can no longer be bought and sold. The corrupt phenomenon of cronyism is no longer possible.

The government's political power is constitutionally limited solely to the protection of individual rights. That is, it is limited to the exercise of retaliatory force against anyone who would initiate force against others. Government has no other power.

A business's economic power can legitimately grow as large as that business is able to grow it, providing it does not violate the rights of others. But never can a business use its economic power to purchase political power. There no longer exists that kind of political power to be purchased. The shelves are empty.

Thus a business, now in this coercion-free environment, cannot use government to force others to trade with it, while excluding competition. As history gives witness, such coercive monopolies were only possible when government was allowed to intervene in the economy.

Positives Realized: There is another side to the coin, namely, the positives realized by eliminating the above evils. These include spectacular prosperity, unimaginable advances in every sector of the economy, and nearly full employment as a steady state.

Some unemployment always exists in a dynamic economy, as inefficient or outmoded enterprises meet their demise. But now unemployment is temporary while failed companies re-tool or turn to other ventures. It is a world made for venture capitalists. Innovation has never been more rampant.

All this barely scratches the surface. It does not touch on the Mars colony, or the development of long-term remission techniques for all cancers, or the pristine nature of the environment, or the longer and healthier life-spans. All these advances have been accelerated by the massive shift of wealth from the public sector back to the private sector, where it was produced in the first place. Government is now one tenth the size it was during its heyday in earlier centuries.[142]

Government funding has become one of the greatest areas of creativity and innovation. The age-old tax system of wealth expropriation and redistribution has been replaced. The vast regulatory state is no more. Entitlement programs are gone. The flow of wealth back to the private sector truly has been astronomical. Again, all this barely scratches the surface.

The Intangibles: There has been a widespread return of the virtue of individual responsibility. This was a virtue that predominated during America's First Enlightenment. At the same time, magnanimous goodwill has become widely evident.

As entitlement programs were phased out, an American population that had become so dependent on them was transformed. Mean-spiritedness as a result of being dependent, and mean-spiritedness as a result of being forced to finance the dependent, have both been supplanted.[143]

It came as a great surprise to many Americans, but the genuinely needy have never been better cared for, despite the fact that people are no longer forced to help them. Rather, the help comes quite naturally.[144]

Volunteerism, always a great phenomenon in America, has skyrocketed. People have more leisure, earlier retirements, shorter work days, longer vacations. We have seen a proliferation of third party administrators (TPA's) promoting and managing volunteer endeavors. These are themselves largely staffed by volunteers. Such TPA's have always existed in America, but now the scale is unprecedented.[145]

Of course, a negative note remains. There are those who perversely seek to live a life of dependence, living off of others, barely lifting a hand to help themselves. Even these, however, find benefactors willing to help. There are always those who are convinced, not only that self-sacrifice is the greatest virtue, but that such virtue is even greater the more *un*deserving the recipients. Such "benefactors" are always free to live their lives of self-sacrifice.

FURTHER RESULTS

Doctrine of Original Sin Marginalized: Now, in America's Second Age of Reason, belief in the innate weakness and depravity of human nature (tenet one of the Post-Enlightenment mindset) is dramatically reduced. There has been a pronounced return of social grace, self-respect, and self-confidence. Optimism and goodwill predominate, along with a search for excellence in all things.

Christianity's doctrine of original sin has become the minority view. The view that humans are inherently weak and depraved is now commonly regarded as *itself* depraved. It is seen as unworthy of humans.

This dramatic about-face in man's view of human nature is not hard to understand. First, widespread depravity was eliminated with the elimination of the evils cited above. Historically, those evils—to religious and secular authority figures—were taken as evidence of the inherent weakness and depravity of human nature. That evidence no longer exists. The system that enabled humans to choose and profit from weakness and depravity is now gone.

Second, Christianity's unreason, discussed at length in chapter five, no longer plays so dominant a role in America. Religion has fallen out of favor during America's Second Enlightenment. As in America's First Enlightenment, *enlightenment* means to be enlightened by *reason*.

Of course, Christian unreason still exists. Freedom of conscience is always a basic right. People are free to believe what they wish to believe. But incursions of religion into politics have now been stopped. Now, religion really *is* strictly a matter of private conscience. No longer are major party platforms vehicles for the agendas of the religious Right or Left. The government no longer has the power to advance those agendas. Church-state separation truly is complete.

Inherent-Depravity-of-Government-View Marginalized: Throughout the 21st century and for much of the 22nd, it was common for libertarian groups to be influenced by this view. To various degrees, they held that a one-government system unavoidably initiates coercion against the citizens of a country. This thinking extrapolated the inherent-depravity-of-man doctrine to an inherent-depravity-of-*government* doctrine.[146]

Now in America's Second Enlightenment, however, belief in this doctrine, like that of Original Sin, has been dramatically reduced. America's new government is properly limited by what is essentially a new constitution.

This constitution explicitly articulates the separations needed to prevent the government from initiating force against any American citizen. All areas of the private sector are now "no fly zones" for government. These are the economy, finance, education, medicine, science, and religion.

There still exist those who hold to the inherent-depravity-of-government doctrine, and the inevitable anarchy it leads to. But proponents of this doctrine, now in America's Second Age of Reason, have been marginalized.

The Vital Role of Government

Securing and Defending Individual Rights: One might conclude from the above paragraphs that government's importance in Second Enlightenment America has been undercut. But actually, just the opposite has been the case.

Yes, for the first time, government is explicitly, *consistently,* limited to the protection of individual rights. But respect for government has never been higher.

Now the prevailing view is that few things are more vital than serving in the defense of individual rights. There is a great awareness that, in the complex culture of an advanced society within a global economy, the defending of individual rights is a daunting task.

The challenges of protecting individual rights are unrelenting and complex. The government, of necessity, has needed to be active, strong, and decisive.

Foreign Policy: America's foreign policy, now in her Second Enlightenment, stands as a model to the world. America leads by example, and she leads by her powerful defense system.

She leads by her unhesitating articulation that the moral stature of a social system is a function of how free it is. She leads by her articulation that the more a country is based on unreason, coercion, and contempt for rights, the more evil it is.

Multiculturalism, the view that all cultures are somehow of equal moral stature, has been recognized as, *itself*, devoid of moral stature.[147]

Immigration: In America's Second Enlightenment, she has again become pro-immigration. The hostility to immigration that was so common in the late 20th century and throughout the 21st is now gone. During that dismal period, American law had largely and tragically prohibited immigration.

Now however, that has changed. America is once again a nation of open immigration. Open immigration is now seen as—not only *politically* right—but *morally* right. Traditional arguments against it have been thoroughly discredited.[148]

Maintaining the Concept of "Rights": During America's Second Enlightenment, the government constantly has had to reassert two vital aspect of the concept, "rights." First, a right is a right to take *action*. It is not a right to a product or service. As pointed out by Ayn Rand last chapter, the latter is a recipe for coercion—the coercion of those who must be forced to provide that product or service.

Second, only *individuals* possess rights. That is, federal and state and local governments do not possess rights, only the people do.[149]

A Sacred Honor: Each sector of government—the police, the court system, the three political branches, the military—involves work that is critical to the wellbeing of a society founded on individual rights. Thus government employment is not only greatly attractive to motivated men and women of ability, for whom individual rights are supreme values, it is also honorable.

As always, government employees swear an oath of office to defend and uphold the constitution of the United States of America. But now this oath, instead of ending with "So help me God," ends with the same two words that ended the 1776 Declaration of Independence. New "inductees" into government now "mutually pledge," in spiritual union with all who preceded them, their *sacred honor*.

Never before has the role of government been made *sacred*. Never before has government been more vital—and honorable—than it is now in America's Second Enlightenment, her Second Age of Reason.

America Today: The Battle for the Human Mind

Transitions: Lengthy transitions will be needed as America evolves to her Second Enlightenment. The above scenario captures only a few elements.

Yet, even for those few, enormous complexities have to be confronted and resolved.[150]

The reversal of a coercive system that has become all but omnipotent needs time. The self-perpetuating nature of chains, both secular and religious, has to be addressed.

Fiscal constituencies, widespread cronyism, and ubiquitous pressure group warfare stand as dead weights against change. To accomplish a reversal, America needs to wrest back an entire country from the forces of unreason. That will require time and effort.

Above all, it will require the recognition that all forces of unreason originate from a political system under which the government has the power to initiate force against its citizens. That is, it will require the realization that government coercion is the root of all social evils, as outlined above.

America's Second Intellectual Revolution: America is a product of revolution. She came into being with a revolutionary war, driven by an intellectual revolution the likes of which had never been seen before. There was the peaceful industrial revolution that followed.

There is her ongoing technological revolution. The potential to improve man's lot in medicine, in education, in living standard, has never been greater than it is now in the 21st century. Truly we live in an extraordinary and exciting time.[151]

But marvelous as this revolution is, it cannot stop, let alone repel, the presence in America of the age-old forces of unreason and coercion. Indeed, today's forces of unreason are themselves skilled exploiters of technology.

The battle for the human mind, by its nature, always needs to be prosecuted at the intellectual level. That battle is well underway. That battle is America's second intellectual revolution and, as we saw last chapter, it was inaugurated in the latter decades of the 20th century by Ayn Rand and her pro-reason philosophy of Objectivism.

The Philosophy of Objectivism

The Ayn Rand Institute (ARI)	Founded 1985. Conduit to all things Objectivist. Register at http://ari.aynrand.org/
Leonard Peikoff	*Objectivism: the Philosophy of Ayn Rand.* 1991. The definitive text, the *only* one.
Harry Binswanger	*The Ayn Rand Lexicon*. Free look-up guide. http://aynrandlexicon.com "Conceptual Index"

Objectivism Applied

Leonard Peikoff	"Why Should One Act on Principle," 1988 address. Ayn Rand Institute eStore. This foundational essay is also available in print in the 2011 *Why Businessmen Need Philosophy.*
Free Market Revolution	Yaron Brook, ARI Executive Director & President and Don Watkins, ARI fellow. 2012.
George Reisman	*Capitalism: A Treatise on Economics.* 1998. www.capital-ism.net
The Objective Standard (TOS)	Quarterly journal, Vol. 1, No. 1 Spring 2006, www.The-ObjectiveStandard.com. Daily blog posts. Searchable on a wide array of topics. Journal articles available as PDF downloads.
20 Top Objectiv-ist Blogs	http://thenearbypen.blogspot.com/2009/04/objectivist-blog-directory.html

Three Battlefields for the Human Mind

The battle for the human mind is a battle for *reason*. It is a philosophic battle. In prosecuting it, three theatres are among the most vital: education, religion, and history.

Education: Throughout history, dictators have recognized that to control a population, you must shape the *mind* of the population. The population must be rendered compliant. You do not want people thinking for themselves; these are the people who defy authority. As C. Bradley Thompson (see below, under "Education") demonstrates, a compliant citizenry has always been an explicit goal of America's government education system. Its architects make that clear. The Thompson essays are fundamental to understanding the role of education in the battle for the human mind.

Religion: Freedom of religion is a basic right, and America is the first nation to prohibit a state religion in its constitution. Many good people, *religious* people, champion liberty, but, unfortunately, do so by appeal to God and the supernatural. Without realizing it, they therefore stand philosophically opposed to liberty. "Religion vs. America," below, explains. This Leonard Peikoff address is fundamental to grasping the adverse role of religion in the battle for the human mind.

History: A return to a culture of reason will necessarily entail a return to respect for history. This includes not only a respect for American history generally, but the history of capitalism specifically. It also needs to include the place of Ayn Rand in the history of philosophy. Today, she continues to be vilified and distorted, as she was during her life, usually by those relying on commentary and interpretation by her avowed enemies. These later-generation detractors continue to ignore readily-available sources (table below and chapter six above), and, quite deliberately, perpetuate the error and distortion.

Regarding the history of capitalism, Rand's 1967 essay collection, *Capitalism: The Unknown Ideal,* does much to set the record straight. See below.

Education	C. Bradley Thompson, "Education in a Free Society," with pointer to his earlier essay on the same subject. http://www.theobjectivestandard.com/issues/2013-winter/education-in-a-free-society.asp.
Religion	Leonard Peikoff, "Religion vs. America," 1986 address. Penetrating indictment of American religion as a destructive force standing against capitalism, rights, and human nature. Full text available on the ARI user page. MP3 download https://estore.aynrand.org/p/114/religion-vs-america-mp3-download.
History	Ayn Rand, *Capitalism: The Unknown Ideal*, 1967 essay collection, largely historical. See especially "Notes on the History of American Free Enterprise" (discussed in chapter six, above) and the lead essay "What is Capitalism?"

The Power of Reason

Reason in World History: History provides overwhelming evidence of the power of reason and thought to advance human life. Throughout history, reason has lavishly rewarded those cultures in which it was a preeminent feature: the Golden Age of Greece, the Renaissance, the European and American Enlightenments. In such periods, reason brought man relative peace, prosperity, intellectual and artistic development, and advance in science.

The Arab world, too, had its Golden Age, from roughly the 8th to the 12th centuries. As scholar Andrew Bernstein recounts, during this era, the Arab rediscovery of Greek thought led to towering achievement—in medicine, literature, mathematics, and astronomy. Tragically, for reasons Bernstein makes clear, the Islamic world ultimately rejected reason, after which it "collapsed into a cultural Dark Age, where it remains." [152]

Indeed, throughout history, every culture driven by unreason has been implacably punished by the coercion to which it inevitably leads. Recall the theocratic dictatorship of Europe's medieval era and the fascist and Nazi dictatorships during the 20th century. Force ruled, mankind suffered—unspeakably.

Consider the history being written today. Note the socialist and fascist dictatorships in Africa. Observe the theocratic dictatorships of the Middle East. Recall the satellite photos of the Korean peninsula at night, lit by the torch of Prometheus in the South but blanketed by darkness in the North, with the exception of its capital city, Pyongyang.[153]

Observe the vast areas of the globe that do not know the light of reason—or modernity. As always, in the absence of reason, and of what reason makes possible, human life languishes—again, unspeakably.

History's record is inescapable. Reason and thought have been the drivers of all human achievement, progress, and flourishing. Aeschylus's Prometheus pointed this out nearly three millennia ago. Ayn Rand declared it in the 20th century and, further, validated reason against all who would subvert it.

Reason in America's History: America's founding documents attest to the power of reason in the creation of a new nation on a virgin continent. With their reason-based formulations, their rights-advancing content, their passionate and decisive phrasing, these documents remain revered by most Americans to this day. It is no coincidence that the Freedom Tower at One World Trade Center, New York City, replacing the Twin Towers lost on September 11, 2001, stands 1776 feet tall, in symbolic tribute to the date of America's *Declaration of Independence*.

America's founding documents remain unique and unprecedented; most Americans, rightly, remain proud of them, despite the wave of multiculturalism swamping the world. As such, they remain foundational in the infrastructure needed for the coming Second American Enlightenment.[154]

Is it reasonable to expect that reason will return to America as a preeminent force? If reality is on the side of reason, that is, if reason *works* in reality, as world history and American history demonstrate so vividly, then the answer should be yes.

Reason in the Individual: Most citizens of the United States of America revere reason, the faculty of observation, logic, and persuasion. They exhibit a natural, emotional defiance when anyone, *abandoning* reason, tries to push them around. They exhibit a healthy contempt for that type of self-serving civil servant whose mission in life seems to be to do just *that*. The Second American Enlightenment will see this emotional defiance mature into an intellectual, *reason-based* defiance.

The very way most Americans carry themselves, the way their bodies move as they go about their daily lives, is cause for optimism. There is the happy confidence of so many of the young, not yet appreciating the power of their minds, not yet fully lit with the power of reason—for the Second Enlightenment is still to come. But again, because they live in America, the basic foundation exists for that to happen—eventually.[155]

Reason-Based Catalysts: Catalysts will accelerate the journey to America's Second Age of Reason. Ayn Rand's philosophy of *Objectivism* is, of course, the greatest catalyst. And many other catalysts now exist to advance and accelerate the intellectual revolution she initiated. Catalysts are ongoing and can take a number of forms.[156]

There are the books to be written and organizations to be formed that will join those already in existence. Together, they will relentlessly promote and accelerate the life-advancing record of individual rights, free enterprise, and liberty.

For economist, George Reisman, there will, of necessity, be the creation of a *Capitalist Party*, "formally organized" and serving primarily as an "educational institution." It will have book-publishing houses and theoretical journals. It will have magazines on current issues and "schools turning out intellectual leaders thoroughly versed in economic theory and political philosophy."[157]

There will likely be an organization focusing exclusively on epistemology, perhaps calling itself *The Epistemology Society*. This would be a group of intellectuals who take on the mission of guarding against and countering bad epistemology. They would directly confront junk science, ignorance of logical fallacies, and widespread manipulation of statistics in order to make falsehoods plausible.[158] The Society will make epistemology exciting—and respectable. Epistemology—the branch of philosophy that studies the nature, origin, means, extent, and certainty of human knowledge—for the first time, will enter mainstream American culture.[159] People will naturally experience delight in using their minds in this "new" way.

There will likely be an organization focusing on constitutional law, perhaps calling itself *The James Madison Constitution Society* in honor of America's great Founding Father. Its long-term mission would be to undo and then reverse the calamitous corruption of America's original constitution which started, as we noted earlier, before the ink was even dry.[160]

There will be the men and women of towering accomplishment, idealism, and integrity, fully committed to the pro-reason philosophy of Ayn Rand, and willing to serve in public office. There will be the likely individuals, in the mold just described, who become president of the United States.[161]

Then there are financial catalysts. There will no doubt be the influx of billion dollar contributions on a regular basis into the pro-reason organizations already formed and yet to be formed.

Reason is Invincible: Reason is self-reinforcing. It is on the side of what is right. It works in reality—always. Philosopher Andrew Bernstein captures it well. "[T]he human capacity to reason," he states, "and the yearning for freedom and prosperity, will survive as long as humanity itself; no degree of irrational philosophy or repressive government will suffice to stamp these out."[162]

Sacred Honor

America's Original Spirit Recovered: America's original spirit was an intellectual defiance of the twin tyrannies of Christian God and coercive government. An unstoppable force, its expression took a number of forms. In the age-old conflict between reason and coercion, it championed reason. In the perennial conflict between the individual and the collective, it upheld the individual. In the irreconcilable defiance-compliance dichotomy, it utterly shunned compliance.

Today, reason-based defiance is shared by all those who work for America's Second Enlightenment, America's Second Age of Reason. For all these "worthies," that spirit of defiance is once again the animating force. For all of them, the torch of Prometheus symbolizes not only intellectual defiance, but a raging fire in the belly. Truly they have recovered America's original spirit—and the sacred honor that goes with it.[163]

There is, however, a vital difference. Today's intellectual revolutionaries seek to advance a philosophy, Ayn Rand's *Objectivism*, that makes explicit certain key areas that were only implicit in America's original founding documents. Just as important, Rand's philosophy addresses the many vulnerabilities in the thinking of Enlightenment intellectuals. As we saw in chapter two, it was these shortfalls that led to the rapid demise of the Enlightenment in Europe and then America.

Ayn Rand's philosophy, in addressing them, is thoroughly reason-based—grounded in human nature, that is, grounded in what man needs to survive and flourish. That is, it is objectively derived from observation, and reasoning on the basis thereof. It is neither subjectively derived, nor supernaturally based. It is the only philosophy that fully defies the tyrannies of unreason—both from government and from God—and can do so long term.

Man Re-humanized: During the 19th century, as the Enlightenment waned in America, an age-old mindset resurfaced and persists to this day. Its tenets, regarding a) the alleged inherent weakness and depravity of human nature, and b) self-sacrifice as the only measure of success, basically dehumanize man. They strip men and women of the self-esteem needed to defy tyrannical authority and set them up, instead, for compliance.

America's Second Enlightenment, her Second Age of Reason, will return humans to their rightful stature. No longer will man be viewed as unnatural, as an enemy of nature, as a marauder on the planet. No longer will man be viewed as inherently weak and depraved. No longer will humans be viewed as creatures to be sacrificed.

Authorities will always exist who seek to force compliance on the individual. In other words, the conflict between defiance and compliance is perennial. Although that conflict will be much abated in the Second Enlightenment, intellectual defiance, that is, *reason-based* defiance, must be preserved. Eternal vigilance against the forces of coercion must be maintained.

In America's Second Enlightenment, the natural world in general, and human nature in particular will be returned to the stature they enjoyed during America's First Enlightenment. Human nature will be supremely valued—perhaps not by everyone, but surely by the movers and shakers in the culture who will sweep up the majority of others.

Ayn Rand's soaring view of human nature and its potential will prevail. Human nature will be recognized as an integration of body and mind, of the physical and the spiritual. And the material realm as a whole, in all its sensual glory, will be recognized as the greatest realm because it includes matter that is animated by consciousness, by reason, by thought, by values, by the spiritual—that is, because it includes human beings—*human* nature.

On such a view of nature and of man, vital concepts historically expropriated by religion, and monopolized by it through the ages, will be snatched back. They will be brought back from an imaginary supernatural realm and returned to where they belong, namely, to man in this *earthly* realm. These are such concepts as ecstasy, exaltation, reverence, worship, rapture, the spiritual, the holy, and the sacred.[164]

The Prometheus Connection: Since his birth in Ancient Greece, Prometheus has stood as the supreme icon of defiance. And together, Prometheus and Zeus bring to life and dramatize that great conflict in human history—defiance versus compliance.

The mythical Prometheus endured diabolical punishment for thousands of years, yet he remained defiant. His final three words in Aeschylus's great drama ring down to us through the millennia, "I am wronged!" This is the Prometheus of the invincible spirit. This is the Prometheus who refuses to surrender, refuses to comply. This is the spirit of America's Founders.

And today, this is the invincible spirit of all who defiantly fight to break the chains of coercion in today's world—again, pledging as they do so, that greatest of pledges—**their *sacred honor*.**

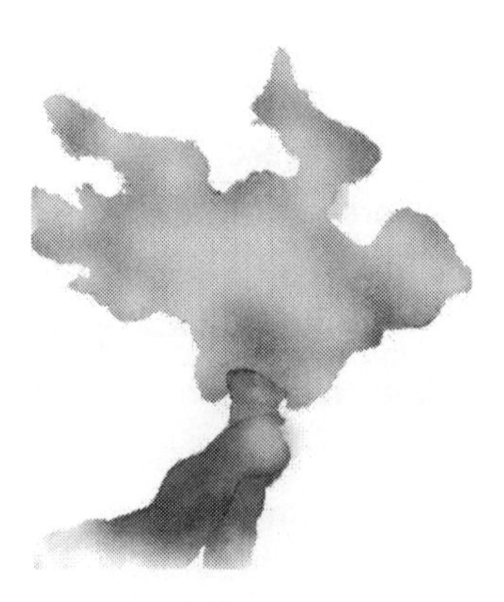

Epilogue

And after Prometheus was unbound from his chains he returned to earth to continue animating mankind with the fire. I speak of the fire of reason and thought. This is the fire that provides the vision for great and daring and defiant achievement. Many are those throughout history who abandoned the fire or sought to subvert it. Many are those who have refused to recognize its supreme efficacy. But Prometheus always prevails in the end, for reason and the good—and greatness of spirit—are invincible.

Excerpt, imagined,
from *Prometheus Unbound*,
lost to history

---

140 Not discussed in this book were the three millennia of Egyptian civilization that preceded Ancient Greece. See again Edith Hamilton's *The Greek Way*, op. cit., pp. 9-14. That period was largely, as she demonstrates by contrasting it with the Golden Age of Athens, three millennia of unreason.

141 The introduction of explicit clauses that strictly separate government not only from religion, as in America's original constitution, but from all areas of the private sector are among the key changes. This means the economy, finance, education, science, and medicine as well. More on this later in the chapter.

142 The Mars colony provided vital emotional fuel for the arduous journey to America's Second Enlightenment. As a concept, it started life with a consortium of visionaries, each of whom was fully committed to pure capitalism and the philosophy of Capitalism's greatest advocate ever—Ayn Rand.

Among these visionaries were a number of American millionaires and billionaires. They provided the venture capital and named their revolutionary colony *The Prometheus Frontier*. In the main lobby of its Mars headquarters, visitors saw twelve words from America's revolutionary days that had been deeply chiseled into the wall behind the reception desk. The wall was pale-red Martian crystal, veined with threads of blue-green. The words were: "We have it in our power to begin the world over again."

None of it would even have begun, however, without reason-based defiance. Tyrannical authority, hostile to revolutionary change, existed in many forms. There was the authority of scientific "consensus" that Mars colonization was not possible. There was the authority of social engineering "consensus" that Earth would languish—its problems unsolved. There was international "consensus" that American "imperialism" must not be sanctioned. But such voices could not withstand the reason-based defiance of the *Frontier's* visionaries. With time, the voices of reason trumped those of *un*reason.

With time, the *Prometheus Frontier* was a stunning success. It demonstrated beyond anyone's wildest imaginings that pure capitalism makes nearly anything possible. And *that* was vital emotional fuel in the quest for America's Second Enlightenment—*on Earth itself*.

For a luminous documentary on the exploration and colonization of Mars, see *The Mars Underground*, Orange Dot Entertainment, 2011, https://www.youtube.com/watch?v=RRiln3gSGGM. Also see, "Mars Direct," *Wikipedia The Free Encyclopedia*, http://en.wikipedia.org/wiki/Mars_Direct.

143 For individual responsibility during America's First Enlightenment, see Yaron Brook and Don Watkins, "America Before The Entitlement State," Forbes, 1/3/12, http://www.forbes.com/forbes/2012/0116/capital-flows-entitlement-programs-cuts-don-watkins-yaron-brook.html.

144 Even during America's age of unreason, when coercion was rampant, Internet sources regularly reported that voluntary financial aid in America, based largely on benevolent good will, was upwards of a third of a trillion dollars per year. Now, during America's Second Enlightenment, that figure has exploded exponentially.

145 As one example, by the end of the 20th century, more than two thirds of American fire fighters were volunteers. See http://en.wikipedia.org/wiki/Volunteer_fire_department. Last modified July 2, 2014.

146 Without question, the historical evidence for this position was overwhelming. Indeed, there never existed a government that did not initiate force against its citizens.

Even America, with its revolutionary constitution making it the freest country in history, failed to escape the evils of coercive government. We saw this earlier, in chapter five. And if America could not escape those evils, a libertarian's thinking often goes, how could any government escape them?

The simple fact, however, is that America's initial constitution was not as robust as it needed to be.

As constitutional scholar Henry Mark Holzer pointed out, America started to compromise its championship of liberty before the ink was even dry on its ratified 1787-1788 constitution. And the compromises continued in a steady stream from that point.

See Henry Mark Holzer, *The American Constitution and Ayn Rand's "Inner Contradiction,"* (Highlands Ranch, Colorado: Madison Press, 2013).

Holzer gives a gripping and shocking account, to the present day, of the post-ratification history of America's Constitution. The title of his book should not be misconstrued. The contradiction to which Holzer refers lies within the intellectual infrastructure upon which the original constitution was erected, not in Rand herself. In his book's title, he is merely attempting to credit Rand with identifying that contradiction.

147 In an early essay, Ayn Rand presents the essence of foreign policy under a capitalist system. See "The Roots of War," in *Capitalism: The Unknown Ideal,* (New York: Signet paperback edition, 1967), p. 39. The essence, as she explains, is free trade.

148 See Craig Biddle, "Immigration and Individual Rights," *The Objective Standard,* Vol. 3, No. 1, Spring 2008. His essay is invaluable in addressing each of the historical arguments against open immigration. http://www.theobjectivestandard.com/issues/2008-spring/immigration-individual-rights/.

See also Ari Armstrong 7/2/14 *The Objective Standard* Blog entry "Rational Morality Requires Amnesty for Rights-Respecting Illegal Immigrants" at

http://www.theobjectivestandard.com/2014/07/rational-morality-requires-amnesty-rights-respecting-illegal-immigrants/?utm_source=TOS+Commentary+%26+Announce

149 For a lucid treatment of this issue, with reference to James Madison in Federalist Paper 46, see Alexander V. Marriott, "Getting Lincoln Right," *The Objective Standard,* Vol. 9, No. 2, Summer 2014, especially pp. 14-15, "The Right of Secession." http://www.theobjectivestandard.com/issues/2014-summer/getting-lincoln-right/.

150 George Reisman maps out the essentials of what is involved in chapter 20 of his masterwork, *Capitalism: A Treatise on Economics*, (Laguna Hills, California: TJS Books, 1998, 1996, 1990). He makes his entire work of more than 1000 pages available as a free PDF on his website at http://www.capitalism.net/.

(Note: a separate download of "PDFlite" freeware from the Internet eliminates the difficulty of navigating PDF files.) There is no better single source in the field of economics. Reisman's *Capitalism* is vast in scope and informed by a lifetime of study of history's greatest champion of capitalism, Ayn Rand and her philosophy of Objectivism.

151 To get a feel for the dynamism of it all, see Karl G. Kowalski, "Apple's App Revolution: Capitalism in Action," *The Objective Standard,* Vol. 7, No. 4, Winter 2012-2013, http://www.theobjectivestandard.com/issues/2012-winter/apples-app-revolution.asp.

152 Andrew Bernstein, "Great Islamic Thinkers Versus Islam," *The Objective Standard,* Vol. 7, No. 4, Winter 2012, http://www.theobjectivestandard.com/issues/2012-winter/great-islamic-thinkers-versus-islam.asp). Also available as a PDF or MP3 file.

153 Satellite photos of the Korean peninsula can be found on a number of sites. See http://www.dailymail.co.uk/news/article-2566606/North-Koreans-really-kept-dark-Space-Station-picture-shows-isolated-communist-state-completely-devoid-lights.html.

154 This remains the case despite the philosophical errors they contain (such as the view that rights are self-evident, God-given, or natural), and then the later corruption of that which was philosophically correct. For the first, see Craig Biddle, "Libertarianism vs. Radical Capitalism," *The Objective Standard,* Vol. 8, No. 4, Winter 2013-14, http://www.theobjectivestandard.com/issues/2013-winter/libertarianism-vs-radical-capitalism.asp.

For America's later corruption of that which the Founders got correct about rights (that they pertain to actions and not objects or services), see Ayn Rand's discussion, last chapter.

155 Of course, many of today's youths do appreciate the power of their minds and the unique pleasure made possible by their exercise. But the cultural emphasis on service is relentless. Service, the culture tells them, in myriad ways, is the "only measure of success." Translation: success is not a matter of becoming your personal best.

This was discussed at length in chapter four, The Post-Enlightenment Mindset.

156 Catalyst organizations are already legion. Of special note, for instance, is Alex Epstein's "Center for Industrial Progress." See http://industrialprogress.com/get-educated/. And see Epstein's inspiring call to the positive mindset—he calls it "Aspirational Advocacy"—that needs to be a part of any activism, at http://industrialprogress.com/2012/01/13/the-power-of-aspirational-advocacy/

157 Reisman, *op. cit.,* p. 970.

158 Of great use to this society would be Harry Binswanger, *How We Know,* (TOF Publications, 2014).

Re. junk science, there is a huge body of literature taking issue with it, yet the junk continues to grow. The environmental movement, for one major example, has always been a hotbed for it. See Keith Lockitch, "Energy Privation: The Environmentalist Campaign Against Energy" in Debi Ghate and Richard E. Ralston, editors, *Why Businessmen Need Philosophy,* (New York: New American Library, 2011).

Marvelous on the subject of statistics is Darrell Huff's still-available classic *How to Lie with Statistics,* (New York: W. W. Norton & Company, 1954), with pictures by Irving Geis.

159 For this definition of Epistemology, I reach back to Leonard Peikoff's Fall 1968 Philosophy 101 course at Polytechnic Institute of Brooklyn.

160 Of course, the radically revised constitution that will result will not be fail-safe. No constitution can be. But attempted initiation of coercion by government will face constitutional barriers that are most formidable, far more explicitly formidable than the original constitution ratified in 1788.

On the subject of how a proper constitution can control government, see Lewis K. Uhler, *Setting Limits,* (Washington, D.C.: Regnery Gateway, 1989), with a foreword by Milton Friedman.

Of great value in this work is Uhler's treatment of how constitutional change takes place. He illustrates with the attempted "tax limitation/balanced budget amendment," of the 1980's.

It is a fascinating account of how very close America came to passing that constitutional amendment and how it would have limited and significantly rolled back the ever-metastasizing government intervention into the private sector.

161 The key qualifier is fully in "fully committed." Quite a number of politicians—Ronald Regan, Paul Ryan, Ron Paul, to name a few—have expressed familiarity and agreement with some of the ideas of Ayn Rand. But on core issues they are in profound disagreement.

See Ari Armstrong, "Dave Brat and Ayn Rand on Rights and Government," *The Objective Standard Blog,* June 12, 2014. http://www.theobjectivestandard.com/2014/06/dave-brat-ayn-rand-rights-government/.

162 Andrew Bernstein, *Capitalist Manifesto, op. cit.,* p. 394.

163 For a vivid example of that fire, reminiscent of Founding Father, Thomas Paine, see Gen LaGreca, *The Pioneer vs. the Welfare State,* Essays on Liberty in Peril, (Winged Victory Press, 2014). Kindle available.

164 Thomas Jefferson's expression, sacred honor, the last two words of the Declaration of Independence, is a marvelous example.

Prometheus & America
A Unique Connection

The Prometheus Connection **is a brief primer on the essentials of America's history and is unique in connecting that history to the myth of Prometheus the Firebringer. Each element of the myth is a metaphor—a metaphor for a distinct force that shaped and defined America in the past—and continues to do so in the present. There are five such metaphors:**

ZEUS: The great metaphor for authority. In the Prometheus myth, Zeus intends to withhold the fire—the fire of reason and thought—and keep it for himself.

In America today, Zeus is reincarnated in two forms. One form is a government given to tyrannical coercion. The other is the Christian God. Each form suppresses reason and thought.

PROMETHEUS: The great metaphor for defiance of authority. Prometheus brazenly defies Zeus by stealing his fire and bringing it to mankind, thus giving humans the power of reason & thought.

America's Founders, by exercising reason and thought, brazenly defied Zeus in both his modern forms—a government given to tyrannical coercion and the Christian God.

PROMETHEUS'S TORCH: The great metaphor for reason and thought. In the myth, Prometheus declares that his gift of fire made possible all mankind's progress and achievement.

America's Industrial Revolution, underpinned by a revolutionary patent system, held Prometheus's torch of reason high and created with it the greatest country ever seen.

CHAINS: The metaphor for coercion and subjugation. In the great myth, a wrathful Zeus punishes Prometheus by chaining him to a mountaintop where an eagle is to feed on him for all time.

As the Enlightenment faded, Zeus's wrath was seen again. Zeus in his government form chains America with coercive regulation. Zeus as God chains America with Christian unreason.

Heracles: The metaphor for the liberator. In the myth, Prometheus remains bound for a great length of time until Heracles frees him from his chains.

In the 20th century, Ayn Rand, through her philosophy and writing, severed America's chains of coercion and unreason, thereby lighting the path to a second Enlightenment.

****

The above connections bring America's history to life. They heighten the drama of the story and of the spirit that is at its core—the spirit of reason-based defiance.

Afterword: Prometheus In The Arts

Ayn Rand, *Anthem*, 1938: Prometheus is the name adopted by her protagonist, Equality 7-2521, when he finally re-claims for himself the concept "I." "I have read of a man who lived many thousands of years ago," he says, "and of all the names in these books, his is the one I wish to bear. He took the light of the gods and he brought it to men, and he taught men to be gods. And he suffered for his deed as all bearers of light must suffer. His name was Prometheus."

Ayn Rand, *Atlas Shrugged*, 1957: In Rand's masterwork, there is a scene in which Francisco D'Anconia says to Dagny Taggart that he knows who John Galt is. "John Galt is Prometheus who changed his mind," states Francisco. "After centuries of being torn by vultures in payment for having brought to men the fire of the gods, he broke his chains and he withdrew his fire—until the day when men withdraw their vultures."

Peter Paul Rubens painting, *Prometheus Bound* 1611-1612:
http://www.peterpaulrubens.net/prometheus-bound.jsp

Most artworks of Prometheus depict him in chains, being punished for transgressing into the realm of the gods. This is not surprising in light of the fact that most of these artists, whether Christian or non-Christian, believed that overreaching pride is the great sin. Rubens masterpiece takes the diabolical punishment two steps further. Not only is the eagle tearing out Prometheus's liver, he is raking his groin with one set of talons and his eyes with the other.

Paul Manfield sculpture, *Prometheus as Fire-Giver*, fountain at Rockefeller Center, 1934:

http://www.bluffton.edu/~sullivanm/newyork/newyorkcity/manship/4298.jpg

Manfield's Prometheus is vulnerable, fragile, and weak. The jagged mountain toward which he is falling suggests the earth, the rectangular pool the ocean, and the ring filled with zodiac symbols the heavens. The Aeschylus quote cut into the red granite background is well chosen: "Prometheus, Teacher in Every Art, Brought the Fire That Hath Proved to Mortals a Means to Mighty Ends." All these elements are intended to suggest the cosmic scope of the myth, but the main subject, Prometheus, visually fails to measure up.

Heinrich Fueger, Prometheus Brings Fire to Mankind, 1817:

http://commons.wikimedia.org/wiki/File:Heinrich_fueger_1817_prometheus_brings_fire_to_mankind.jpg

This luminous image comes closest to doing justice to the myth. Prometheus lifts his torch high, setting the sky on fire as if by the sun, before touching it down to the figure in shadows—mankind prior to reason. Prometheus's pose and face express defiance, with a touch of apprehension in the face. But the apprehension is attenuated by his raised and thoughtful left hand. It is as if he were saying to Zeus, "I know you do not want me to do this, but it is the right thing to do; I am going to do it." Fueger's masterpiece is visually reminiscent of Ayn Rand's description of Kira's Viking early in *We the Living,* standing on a tower above a city he has conquered. And as he raises a goblet of wine into the first rays of the coming sun, he salutes, "To a life which is a reason unto itself."

About the Author

Kevin Osborne was born in 1941 and educated in Brooklyn and New York City. Currently, he lives with his wife, Judy, on a back country road in Connecticut.

He started college as an engineering major. But, having a life-long interest in literature and philosophy, he regularly sampled humanities courses as electives at the Polytechnic Institute of Brooklyn, now Polytechnic Institute of New York University. It was here that he discovered a gifted philosophy teacher, Leonard Peikoff, whose passion for the subject of philosophy Osborne found absolutely infectious. Irresistibly drawn to this inspired teacher, who taught many philosophy courses at Polytechnic, a change of major to English (Humanities) followed. This led to graduate school and in 1979 Osborne graduated from the City University of New York with a Ph.D. in Philosophy. His doctoral dissertation, "Aristotle's Conception of Megalopsychia," dealt with that giant's theory of the nature and origin of "greatness of soul." (This has inspired his most recent works, *Mutekikon* and *The Prometheus Connection*.)

Following graduate school, Osborne worked mainly in the field of Quality Engineering. The first half of his career was in the private sector and the second half was in the Department of Defense. As a sideline, he was contributing editor for Freshwater and Marine Aquarium Magazine for several years during the 1980's and 1990's. His specialty was planted freshwater aquariums, and he wrote many articles for like-minded aquarium enthusiasts.

Kevin Osborne now works as a writer and artist. He is the author-illustrator of the 2010 fable, *Mutekikon*, a picture-storybook on DVD, about man's indomitable spirit. His 2014 *The Prometheus Connection* is his latest book, for which his painting, "The Torch of Reason," appears on the cover.

Osborne can be reached at kevin@prometheusconnection.com for more information about his art, DVD, and books. Go to the back of this book for samples of his artwork and details of his *Mutekikon* DVD."

Index

E

F

G

H

I

J

K

S

T

U

W

Z

Art Prints by Kevin Osborne

"Bridges"

Art Prints by Kevin Osborne

"No-Yes"

Kevin Osborne is a writer / artist living in North-Central Connecticut. As an artist, he has worked in Ink Wash and in Watercolor for more than 30 years.

He makes his art available as high quality giclée, limited-edition prints, framed and ready to hang.

Galleries for Argentine Tango, Inkscapes, Capescapes, and other. All framed prints $69.99 which includes shipping.

Place all orders on line. Simply enter "**Mutekikon–Etsy**" into your browser to find link to his shop. Shipment within 1 to 2 days.

The Invincible Spirit
Mutekikon the DVD

The Invincible Spirit
Mutekikon the DVD

In *Mutekikon* the DVD lavish, atmospheric images come alive with subtle camera effects adding depth, elongating time, suggesting movement.

Nature sounds, evocative native style flute, and voice narration further take the viewer inside these images – into the captivating, haunting, meditative realm of *Mutekikon*.

Discover Invincible Spirit

FEATURES

- Audience: All ages, 8 and up
- 16:9 Widescreen, NTSC, Region Free
- Progressive Scan
- Stereo
- Dynamic Text
- Language: English
- Subtitles: English, Spanish
- Extras: Trailer, Players, Scenes
- 25 minutes
- Monochromatic
- Available only on DVD

Original Story:
Written, illustrated & narrated by Kevin Osborne
Original Music:
Composed & performed by Malcolm Shute
Audio & Video Production:
Michael Spooner, The Tuning Spoon

The Invincible Spirit
Mutekikon the DVD

Mutekikon, the DVD, is a fictional expression of Kevin Osborne's 1979 doctoral dissertation in Philosophy, "Aristotle's Conception of Megalopsychia" (Greatness of Soul).

This exalted spirit, whether it goes by the name *mutekikon* or *megalopsychia*, is the same spirit possessed by all those to whom *The Prometheus Connection* is dedicated. That is, it is the spirit of all those who champion, and have *ever* championed, *reason-based defiance*.

*Mutekikon** is a short fable of less than 1000 words set in 8th century Hokkaido. It was written and illustrated by Osborne with monochrome ink wash paintings and published on DVD in 2010. It tells the story of a rare eagle and a boy who have bonded to triumph over a great evil and over fear itself.

In this 25 minute production, Osborne's lavish atmospheric paintings come alive with subtle camera effects adding depth, elongating time, and suggesting movement. Nature sounds, evocative native style flute, and voice (the author's) further take you inside the images—into the captivating, haunting, meditative realm of *Mutekikon*.

Experience this world—experience the magic. Order on Amazon for $6.98 (with shipping). Go to Amazon and simply search on "Mutekikon."

* Muteki (invincible) and kon (spirit) are two Japanese concepts originally conjoined by the author to bring into being this powerful and unique name.

Made in the USA
Charleston, SC
13 January 2015